NOTES FROM THE NORTH POLE

Emily Maguire is a British singer-songerwriter best known for her strong, thought-provoking lyrics and supremely expressive voice. Since the release of her debut album *Stranger Place* in 2004, her songs have been played regularly on BBC radio and have won her fans across the globe. She recorded her first two albums in Australia where she spent four years living on a goat farm in a shack made out of wood, tin and potato sacks, making and selling goat cheese to finance her music. Following her return to the UK to tour with Don McLean and release her third album *Believer*, Emily published *Start Over Again*, a highly personal account of her experiences of living with bipolar disorder. In between tours, she has performed many gigs in mental health hospitals in the UK, singing her songs about surviving mental illness for staff and patients. *Notes From The North Pole* is a collection of writings based on her journals, her poems and her song lyrics.

Also by Emily Maguire

BOOKS

Start Over Again

RECORDS

Stranger Place
Keep Walking
Believer
Bird Inside A Cage
A Bit Of Blue

NOTES FROM THE NORTH POLE

A Collection of Poetry, Prose and Songs

EMILY MAGUIRE

First published in 2016
by Emily Maguire

FIRST EDITION

ISBN 978 0 9566801 2 9

Printed and bound by CPI Group (UK) Ltd, Croydon, CR0 4YY

Thanks to Ruth Sharman and Alison Paine
for reading my original manuscript and giving me
such helpful, positive feedback.

I dedicate this book to Christian Dunham,
my compass when I was lost at the north pole.

CONTENTS

PART 1

PART II

PART III

PART I

IN EVERY SKY

I wait for time to unfold, like a road going over a hill. I can see where I'm going, I can see where I've come from, I can walk fast or I can walk slow, I can look around me, I can look up at the space above me. And without questions, without answers, I will know who I am and why I am here, and how to make the most of every grain of sand pouring through my hourglass. In every grain, a beach. By every beach, an ocean. Above every ocean, a sky. In every sky, a sun.

BACK HOME *(from the album 'Keep Walking')*

I'm one drop in a sunlit sky
Where seagulls fly, they rise and fall
I can't stop now a cloud is flying
The sky is crying and the seagulls call
Now I go with the river, go where the river goes
And I flow with the river, I know what the river knows

I sit still in the sound of silence
And feel the fire in my eyes and ears
And I know there's no point in violence
Fear and fighting only ends in tears
So I go with the river, go where the river goes
And I flow with the river, I know what the river knows

That I will rise up with the sun
And I will fall down with the rain
And I will flow like a river goes
Back from where I came
Back home, back home

But time moves me on, I keep moving on
Life moves me on

It's high tide and the moon is rising
And clouds are dancing for the dying day
In a blue sky where the birds are flying
The clouds are crying, I can hear them say
Go with the river, go where the river goes
Flow with the river and know what the river knows

And you will rise up with the sun
And you will fall down with the rain
You will flow like a river goes
Back from where you came
Back home, back home

OCEAN

He has the mind of an ocean
it makes me want to dive down deep
see the stillness beneath these wilful waves

SPACE AND TIME

My mind has no boundary, no borderline other than that which I give it. By saying "I want" and "I like", I create a high wall. By saying "I don't want" and "I don't like", I create an opposing high wall. By looking only at these walls and not the space between them I build another wall to make a triangle. And I stand inside this triangle for eons and eons of spaceless time until one day I climb up the third wall and look out at a huge sky and a horizon so far and wide I can only guess that it's there at all. And I look at my walls and realise that all this time I have been suffering for lack of space and lack of time, and suffering for fear of space and fear of time, without realising that there is no space and there is no time.

BEING

Mind is like space
Space is our nature
It is within us
But as soon as we
Experience it, we
Fill it up with
Distractions, things
To see, hear, do
Emptiness does not mean
State of bliss in our
Western tongue
But a vacuum of despair
Heaven is a space inside
A pair of eyes when
You are blind
We've been busy our
Whole lives and most
Of us will die never
Having stopped thinking
And started being

FALLING ON MY FEET *(from the album 'Stranger Place')*

I have a roof above my head
I have a blanket for my bed
I have friends and a lover to keep me warm
And if I only walk the ocean
I'll be strong in my devotion
I'll be falling on my feet to the ground

Cos I had the sky above my head
And I had a doorstep for my bed
But I had friends and a lover to keep me warm
I had everything that money can't buy
A piece of paradise
Cos everything but money can be found

And I've been around and round my head
I've been born and I've been dead
I've been stolen by the keeper to the crown
And I've been raised by the ocean
I've been burned and I've been broken
I've been falling on my feet to the ground

I've been long enough, I've been long enough
I've been lost and I longed to be found

Cos I've been wrong and I've been read
And I had the sky inside my head
And I've been thrown by the keeper to the ground
But if I only walk the ocean
I'll be strong in my devotion
I'll be falling on my knees coming round
Falling from the heat coming down
Falling on my feet to the ground

I MET A MAN

I met a man who told me we are all machines
So where do all the dreams come from?

PRAYER

I am sick of hope, I like prayer better. When there's nothing we can say, and nothing we can do, we pray. We are all waiting for the universe to unfold with all its alarms and surprises and ingenious ways of making everything work out okay until suddenly there's a blip in the programme and you fall down the gap between happiness and survival and all is suffering once more.

So life is suffering but only if you perceive it as such. Not the suffering of animals but the suffering of change depends on our perception. You suffer only if you expect everything to last, love to be constant, the sun to always shine, the rain to always fall. If you have no expectation, if you simply exist in each moment with no pushing or pulling, no yearning for the past or hoping for the future, just watching the rise and fall of each breath with gratitude in your heart, a smile upon your lips and acceptance in your eyes, would that then be nirvana? Nothing changes but nothing is the same?

Then I would know the right words to say, I would have the heart to love all beings without fear or favour, I would have the eyes to see the whole horizon, I would have the ears to hear the fragile beating of my heart, I would know no future, I would have no past, I would be free of every chain I ever locked around myself, I would cut the shadow from my feet, erase the frown from my forehead, place a smile like a sun upon my face, my arms would become an embrace, my hands folded in serenity, in prayer.

GIVE ME SILENCE

Give me silence in the morning
At the ending of the day
Give me reasons to believe in
Give me faith to find my way

WRITING

I'm just writing
For the sake of words
Starting to fall like
Water in my head
Waiting for the tap
To flow fully
To find there is so much
I have to say
I haven't said
Through all this time
Of thinking but not
Writing, clouds build up
Obscure the sun
And all I would have done
Is pick up this pen
And begin somewhere,
Even mid-sentence
Let the words burst through
The dam in my mouth
Saying this is who I am
This is my truth
Is there anyone out there
Who can see it too?

RIGHT THIS SECOND

The songbirds wait for spring to let them sing and the rest of us sit in cold rooms with fires burning in our hearts, not daring to ask questions such as why for fear the answer may be a long dark silence. Around the world people are praying, laughing, making love, dying, right this second. Every moment that passes thousands of people are being kind, being cruel, being hopeful, being afraid. And I have a song in my head and hope in my heart – hope, that crafty saboteur with its long shadow of doubt dragging along behind it.

STANDING *(from the album 'Keep Walking')*

I bend like a reed
Blowing in the breeze
I go with the flow
Where the river wants to go
And my roots are deep, my branches seek
To embrace the wrestling breeze
So winds of change
And godforsaken hurricanes
Won't blow me over

So bring it on, bring it on and I'll stay
Bring it on, bring it on and I'll stay standing

Like a boxer in a ring
I'll keep standing for another round
Held up by string
But I'm no dancing puppet that don't feel a thing
And all I know is fist throws and body blows
Won't bring me down
So don't think it's beating me
I'll just keep blinking as the blows sink in
And I'll be thinking

Bring it on, bring it on and I'll stay
Bring it on, bring it on and I'll stay standing

My paper wings, a piece of string
And pretty things that keep me sane
Unopened doors, and something more
I've said before that calls my name
But I'm still unsure, cos I've had the floor
Pulled out before beneath my feet
But there's safer ground, so tie me down
Try to turn me upside down
And I'll be bound to say

Bring it on, bring it on and I'll stay
Bring it on, bring it on and I'll stay standing

A HANDFUL OF DUST

Hours fall like autumn leaves
You think time grows like fruit on a tree
But you'll return to what you were
A handful of dust in a fragile earth

SUNSET

Walking along the icy cliff path towards a fiery sunset, no-one there but me and the seagulls. And they had nothing to say but plenty to cry about as they whirled up, down and around the waves, the icy grey waves and me high above, walking and walking, all my troubles trying to tag along like feeble shadows as I turned to face the fire of the setting sun.

HYPNOTISED

I walk across the ocean in my mind
There is no shore as far as I can see
Just floating in this universe of time
So many things I want that I don't need

I'm grateful for the stars and northern lights
Not all illusions are so beautiful
I wish that I could hold them in my sights
Capture the flow, but mind's so mutable

And silence has a voice that I can hear
When all the sirens stop and I can breathe
Words of wisdom whisper in my ear
The true reflection of the truth in me

The sun is gold in these darkened days
We've eyes to wonder but we've lost our way
To have and hold until the journey's end
When at last we go under, we're hypnotised again

SALT WATER

Fulfilling
desire is
like drinking
salt water
A whole ocean
is not enough
to quench
your thirst

TURNER

At 8 o'clock the birds stopped singing but not because of the dusk – the sun was still clinging to the clouds. And I was standing there in that blue and pink sweater you gave me, staring at the sky like I thought it might disappear if I blinked. But it was still there, distant, but magnificent, like a huge Turner high on the wall at the National Gallery, but only me there to see it.

THE WHEEL

Wanting things to be
Other than what they are
Is what keeps the wheel
Turning and the fires
Burning. If I could
For one second be
Content, not grasping
Not pushing away
Would I realise that everything
Is as it should be
There is no good or bad
Only arising and non-arising
I would be grateful
Whichever of the two occurred
To love and learn

GETTING OLDER *(from the album 'A Bit Of Blue')*

I've a story here to tell
Of a child who did so well
All her dreams were gonna save her
It was all bright lights and movie stars
Looking cool in cars
Getting older something changed her

But once upon a time everybody lived happy ever after

But every dream day turned to dust
And only lies we learn to trust
Getting older something changed us
Of all the things I'd thought I'd be
The only one still here is me
Getting older we're just changing

But once upon a time everybody lived happy ever after
Once upon a time everybody lived happy ever after

But I've a story still untold
I'll still be young before I'm old
Getting older nothing changes
I'll still be waiting and wanting more
Filling time I've filled before
Getting older nothing changes

But once upon a time everybody lived happy ever after
Once upon a time everybody lived happy ever after
Whatever happened after

But it was all bright lights and movie stars
Looking cool in cars
And getting older nothing changes

BEING STILL

All air is one. Non-physical objects have no sides, no edges, no walls, no barriers. They are not defined by boundaries. They do not label themselves as 'objects' – separate and divisible into many, infinite parts which ultimately end up as particles of emptiness only visible, only existing, as and when you observe them. So I could build a castle in the air and live in it. My mind believes it has walls and a drawbridge and a moat, and rows of frightened soldiers to defend it – for there must be an enemy or why would you bother having defences?

The Buddha sat cross-legged on the ground beneath a big tree and he placed his hand upon the ground and said I will not be moved from this spot until I have attained enlightenment. And he did. That says much for the importance of being still. A bit like a pool of water: if it is still, it becomes like a mirror and you can recognise yourself in it. You can see yourself for what you really are. And what you really are is a space-time machine carrying the most precious treasure of all – consciousness, the spark.

THE BORDERLINE *(from the album 'Stranger Place')*

Where is the borderline
The boundary between your tribe and mine
Are we the rain, the river, the cloud and the sea
If we are like water then which drop is me?

And what is time - the fast blink of an eye
A circle so vast that we think it's a line?
And what is space - the air, the silence we breathe
A place of our own and the ghosts we don't see

Is it the boundary, the borderline
Between you and I, your mind and mine?

Is fire the spark, the fuel, the air or the heat
The smoke in your eyes or the ash at your feet
Are trees the root, the branch, the wood or the leaves
The forest we burn or the broom that we keep

Beneath the stairs, the stars, the space in a jar
The air outside is that where you are?
Is that the borderline, the boundary
Between you and I, between your tribe and mine?

But isn't fear the dark shadow of hope
The things that we want and the things that we don't
And so we cling and close the eyes that look in,
The soul we don't see under the skin

Cos that's a boundary, the borderline
Between you and I, between your tribe and mine

But we both were born and both will die
And in between will doubt and dream
Of a better life than life before
A meaning or a reason for

This feeling of being different, defined
When we are only dreaming
Of boundaries and borderlines
I hope we wake up

Cos what is love - a word, the feeling of you
Something we dream or the things that we do?
And who am I - these thoughts, this feeling, my views
A fragile form or a dreamer like you?

Are we so different, defined
Where is the borderline?

When we are like water, like trees
We have a name, an illusion of identity
Of boundaries, of borderlines
But my dreams are yours
And your fears are mine

I hope we wake up from this dream
Of being different, defined
When we are only space and time
Space and time

THE SUN

The sun behind the cloud is worth more than any silver lining.

LIFE LESSONS

I've been lost
It taught me how to find my way
I've been a fool
It taught me how to be wise
I've been cruel
It taught me to be kind
I've been fearful
It taught me to be brave
I've been hasty
It taught me to bide my time
I've been crazy
It taught me to be sane
I've been wrong
It taught me not to judge
I've been in pain
It taught me empathy
I've been angry
It taught me to think before I speak
I've been deaf
It taught me how to listen
I've been blind
It taught me how to see
I've been burned
It taught me not to touch the fire
I've been heartbroken
It taught me how to love
I've been happy
It taught me how to cry
I've been young
It taught me to grow old
I've been dead
It taught me how to live
I've been alive
It taught me how to die

THE FOOL

Every time your ego rears its ugly head, laugh at it. Don't take it seriously. Ego is desperate to be taken seriously. It wants to be put on a big gold throne and bowed to by you. If you just laugh at it and open the door, it is no longer king, but the fool. Yes I am the fool sometimes, but I am also a Buddha dreaming that I am a fool. I want to wake up.

LATER

With the bright light in my eyes
And the smell of the chilled blue sky
Wondering why I'm not moving on
This winter won't last for long

And later, sitting on the train watching
The rail run past with the thoughts
Running fast through my head.
But it was all left unsaid

Cos later, I'd wish I hadn't said the words
Like water falling though my head
I would have built a dam in my mouth
A water wall to stop it coming out

But the spaces move so fast and not a second lasts in a mind
And somewhere a clock is slowly striking out the time
And later, eyes open wide, their restless sight
Keeps watch in the sleepless night

We watched the sun dye the afternoon
And in the light of a laidback moon
We talked of dreams and of innocence
Of all the things that still don't make sense

But later I wished I hadn't said the words
Like water falling through my head
I should have built a dam in my mouth
A water wall to stop it coming out

We'll blow the dust from off our dreams
And find a higher self-esteem
Seek out new horizons to see
Cos there are other ways to be
Cos there are other ways to be
There are other ways

NOW AND THEN

Now turned into then
What if became when
The end had no beginning
The beginning was the end

Grains of time are falling
Through the hourglass of my life

A DIZZYING THOUGHT

There are an infinite number of places I could be right now. If any one of the millions of steps I have taken had been in a different direction, I would be somewhere completely different. It's a dizzying thought. Followed by the thought that there is nowhere I would rather be than here. Followed by the thought that I know I will never be here again – the wheel must turn and I must travel with it. Impermanence is a nice thought when things are tough, and a tough thought when things are nice.

GONE

No-one will think of me
Everything I've known
Everyone I've met
Will cease to exist
Thought of no more
Gone
Like a sunset
Clouds greyed to black
Only stars to light the space
Between, where we used to be
Where I once loved you
And you loved me
And time passed, deluding us
There was ever a future
Without a past
Where we made plans
Like castles in the air
In the space where
Our voices could be heard
Our hands could be held
Our eyes could be met
Our faces recognised
Hearts beating until
The beating stopped

DUST AND AIR

For all my troubles and all my cares
All I was was dust and air

CAREFREENESS

My thoughts are milling around like people in a crowd. Carefreeness. Face the future with carefreeness, with abandon. Be positive, see the sun, not shadows. Nothing and everything. Everything is a big word. So is space and I can fill it with one word, and that word isn't 'God' or 'Love', it's 'Om', which I'm not sure I understand, or rather I am sure I don't understand. But as long as the wheel keeps turning, the cart keeps moving and as long as the cart keeps moving, the wheel keeps turning and all I have to do, sitting pretty up top, is admire the view, and enjoy the ride.

FREE *(from the album 'Believer')*

If I have faith, if I am wise
If I can wait and open my eyes
I won't steal and I don't lie
You can own a hundred houses
But there's nowhere you can hide
And nothing else is holy
Now everything's for sale

But I will be free

If I forgive, if I don't mind
If I can give, if I take my time
I can hope and I can smile
You can only hold the lifebuoy
Kicking for a while
And nothing else is holy
Now everything's for sale

But I will be, oh I will be so free

If I could see and realise
If I could feel a stillness inside
I won't kill cos when I die
You can't buy your soul back
From the salesman in the sky
And nothing else is holy
Now everything's for sale

But I will be, oh I will be so free

TINKER, TAILOR

Tinker, tailor, soldier, spy
I made my bed and here I lie

NORMAL

This morning is the usual cacophony – no that's a complete exaggeration – just a stream of thoughts like everyone else. What! You mean I'm NORMAL? Yes. Sorry to have to break it to you like this, but yes you're normal. Average, ordinary – ordinary as human beings can be, being rather extraordinary beings. I know your ego isn't going to like this but you are pretty much like every other boxed up product on the assembly line of life – no raggedy doll, no premium-priced limited edition. Just an ordinary person. It's what you do that makes you special, not what you are. If you are as kind as you can be, if you are gentle, thoughtful, careful, respectful, humble, generous, helpful, patient, persistent, diligent and courageous, then you have realised your potential to be special but you also probably don't realise that you are because your ego is no longer assessing, criticising, judging, analysing, competing, whining, shouting, pleading, cajoling, manipulating, begging, threatening, coveting and generally wasting your precious time.

PRECIOUS TIME

Waking up each morning
To find time has slipped by
Again.
When I went to sleep
It was August
And now it's March
I can't turn the clock back
Only forward by an hour
Once a year
What would I have done
With that hour?
Composed a song?
Cried?
Precious time we cannot
Pin it down
Make the good times last
The bad ones pass
All in good time
They say
Counting the minutes, the hours,
And the days

PASSING BY *(from the album 'Keep Walking')*

Passing by I caught the eye
Of the child on a back street corner
Waiting for her ride
Her fate sealed in stiletto heels
By a pimp beside her closing deals,
I saw the look in her eye

Passing by I caught the eye
Of the stranger on the escalator
Waiting for his ride
A briefcase for a ball and chain
In a daily rat race for the train
I saw the look in his eye, and it cried

I've been around too long now
I've seen too much wrong yeah
I've had it up to here
I've had it down the years
And I'm not that tough
I think I've had enough

Passing by I caught the eye
Of the woman at the check-out counter
Waiting for her ride
Name-tagged with a smile that sagged
Like the shopping in the plastic bags
I saw the look in her eye, and it cried

I've been around too long now
I've seen too much wrong yeah
I've had it up to here
I've had it down the years
And I'm not that tough, no I'm not that tough
I'm not that tough
I think I've had enough

THE DOOR

I am staring at my shadow and wondering why I can't see the sun. Writing these pages, reading books, am I telling myself all the time "The door is locked, where is the key"? Maybe if I just let go, relax, stop trying to push a square peg in a round hole, maybe I'll find out that not only is the door not locked, but there is no door because there are no walls, and no floor and no ceiling either, nothing there at all. My cell is an illusion of my mind. I can leave anytime I choose.

SOMETHING *(from the album 'Keep Walking')*

Something has appeared
In the corner of my tear-dried eye
Something like a door opening
Or a light I've turned on inside
But I can't see clearly now

And I could never turn around no I
I can only hold the hand of time
And I don't know where it's taking me
Though I'm making these moments in mind
So I can't see clearly now
No I can't see clearly now

And everything is overturned in that
Nothing is permanent, life, oh life
And even as the wheel is turning
The road is running out of sight
So I can't see clearly
No I can't see clearly, clearly now

I want to be free, I want to see clearly
I want to be free and I want to see clearly now

Cos something has appeared
Like a tear in the corner of my eye
Something in the air
I'm so scared of the endless friendless goodbyes
But I can't see clearly now
No I can't see clearly now

THE EDGE

There's an edge
In my head
And I'm standing on it
Trying not to look down
Like a suicide
Who's not sure
And the only thing
To keep me from falling
Is the power of my mind
The belief that this edge
Is in my head

PRIDE VS CONFIDENCE

Pride is a large, extremely ugly monster blocking out the sun. It is best friends with anger and jealousy. It is completely self-serving at the expense of everyone else. "Have a humble mind," the teaching says. I know also I need to have confidence. Confidence is not related to pride. Arrogance is. Confidence is quiet, unshakeable, it stands its ground whether in the spotlight or on the sidelines. Arrogance tramples over set and scenery and other actors in its bid for centre-stage. Pride claps from its box. Arrogance thinks it is owed the world. Confidence knows it is owed nothing and is therefore loved by the world. Confidence knows it has nothing to lose and nothing to gain – confidence in and of itself needs nothing and no-one to justify its existence, so it remains steady, like a candle flame in a cathedral. Pride meanwhile is lighting a bonfire of vanities outside, burning the grass and the trees and the debris of its past achievements and future glories. People watch from a distance. Arrogance warms its hands and gazes goggle-eyed at its reflection in the flames. In the cathedral, it is quiet: silence has the conch. The only sound is that of aspiration, of people's heads bent in prayer, and a glow of faith about their faces, upturned to the huge stained-glass silent window at the end. There is no cross, only confidence. Pride has no place here.

HORNS

One moment
I'm a rabbit in the headlights
The next
I'm a demon breathing fire
And I don't know which
Is really me
Or if one is a front
For the other
Like a solar eclipse
Wanting to be liked
Means constant
Suppression of anything
Untoward
Horns on my head
For example
I flutter the wings
On my back
To try and distract
Attention, grow my hair
Long
But the wind blows
And the tips show through
Though I'm not about
To admit
There's any more than
A tip
So said the captain
Of the Titanic

SAND

I am a grain of sand on a beach five miles wide.

REFUGE

Practise positive thinking was my New Year's resolution. Anxiety is not positive thinking. Confidence is. I try to hold myself still on the shifting sands between too much, and too little. One way leads to the desert, the other to a raging waterfall. How many people are waking up this morning without the will to take another breath, another step? How do they carry on? People with depression and anxiety who turn their pain into anger because they can't express it for what it really is – sadness, confusion, hopelessness, despair. Why do some people get this and others don't? I guess the same reasons some people get diabetes and others don't.

But the thing about suffering is you feel like it will never change, you will always feel this way, your situation will remain as claustrophobic, as dark and frightening as it is this very moment. But you can't nail storm-clouds to the sky - they will rain, they will rain down on you like tears from heaven and you will stand there feeling like you must cry forever but then one day the clouds are gone, all the rain has fallen and the sky is clear. You look up with amazement and see space and sunlight and a whole new horizon. I'm not talking about hope, I'm talking about peace of mind, contentment, being happy to be in the only place you could ever be – right here and right now. Because you understand that clouds come and clouds go, and all you need is a refuge, a refuge from the rain.

GOLDEN AND GORGEOUS

Sitting on the train in the rush-hour, rain
Is running like tears down the windowpane
Passing city lights as the night comes down
Like a tin of sardines the people seem
Sitting reading books and their magazines
Staring at the ceiling, homeward bound
And they sit tight beside each other's lives
And they try not to catch each other's eyes

Billy caught the train in the rush-hour rain
He's hoping to be home by the time the pain
Stabbing in his leg could get him down
And Lily's running late from a job she hates
Thinking how to take money she can't make
Wondering when she's gonna hit the ground
And they sit tight beside each other's lives
But they're alike inside

Cos all they ever really want to be
Is golden and gorgeous, wild and free
Like all the stars in magazines
So golden and gorgeous, wild and free

Jimmy's found a seat and he's fast asleep
He's dreaming of the girl he'd really like to meet
The one who'll never try to bring him down
And Ellie's leaving home for the umpteenth time
She's taken all her clothes from the washing line
She swears she's never going to go back now
And they're alike inside

Cos all they ever really want to be
Is golden and gorgeous, wild and free
Like all the stars they seem to be
So golden and gorgeous, wild and free

Mary has a date at half-past eight
She worries that the train will make her late
Worrying that love will let her down
And Greg is going home to his wife Simone
He's talking to her now on his mobile phone
Hoping she's alone now he's homeward bound
And they sit tight beside each other's lives
And they try not to catch each other's eyes

MIND IS LIKE AN OCEAN

Wind howls, rain falls
Perhaps I should care
But I don't at all

Finished a song and walked down to the wild, windblown
sea. Buddha said mind is like an ocean. That's what mine
looks like then.

THE RUG

I thought I had a handle
On life
I made plans
But life
Had other ideas
And just when I thought
I was in control
The rug was pulled out
From beneath my feet
And I fell
Flat on my face
Now I'm back up again
Standing on another rug
And feeling insecure
Understandably
Perhaps it's better to kneel
Less far to fall

IF YOU COULD SEE

If you could see through this cloud
You'd know the sky's still blue
But the rain has to fall
Before the sun shines on you

ANXIETY

Woke up worrying this morning. Struggling with this song – why 'struggling'? Why not just 'working'? Look at the language you use – words programme our minds. They provoke an emotional response which at a fundamental level is a binary reaction - 'safe' or 'unsafe'. The subconscious seems to only operate those two modes. At the moment, my subconscious is feeling very unsafe so how do I calm it down? Play the part of the headmaster reassuring the caretaker that everything's alright. Because everything is alright and will be alright. Act in control and you will feel in control. Act scared and you will feel scared. I am in control of the choices I make in my life – which choices are offered to me depends on my karma, which again is the result of my own actions – my past choices – so again I am in control of the choices I make.

That's on one level. On another level – how those choices manifest to us – we have no control whatsoever. I can choose how I react. I can choose how I act. I can choose which choice to take. I could be happy, I could be sad, I could be angry, I could be glad. All these states of mind are available to me in any one instant, in the blink of an eye. Anxiety is a habit. It's also a delusion. Anxiety is the way my subconscious thinks it keeps me safe. But by constantly worrying about the next crisis I am prepared for the blow, but unable to relax and enjoy the ride the rest of the time.

I know all this shit, but that doesn't keep the demons at bay – they grab my mind as soon as I awake. I'm sick of living this way. But thoughts are just clouds, I pay them too much heed. I say oh fuck look the sky is grey, it's the end of the world, solid blocks of greyness are going to come crashing down on my head! Then the next day the sky is blue and I am so relieved and grateful which is good but also unnecessary because there was always and forevermore going to be a blue sky following a grey sky *at some point*. What I need to learn to do is not attach an imaginary future to the present moment, like shackling carriages to an engine. The present moment is intangible but manifest. Worry and anxiety rely on the concept of future time – a future where all and any disasters can occur. If I stopped imagining the future, all that fear would disappear. All that 'hope' as well – hope is the wolf in lamb's clothing.

Don't think of tomorrow or next week or next year. Don't think what might or might not happen. Don't think your way out of doing anything with carefree abandon. How about this: stand on a windswept hilltop, there's a wide horizon in front of you, the sky is blessed with white dancing clouds. Open your arms wide, your heart wide open, and say to the universe: "Do with me what you will."

THE DEADLINE

What if I knew the sell-by date on my life
What if I knew I'd one more day alive

Would I light a hundred cigarettes
Sit choking on a chain of life regret,
Why was I so paralysed by fear of heights
Like a rabbit in the headlights, would I?

What if I knew that one more day was my life
What if I knew there's no way out of the night

Would I cry a hundred crucifying tears
Praise my fears for always proving right
I can't defy the hand of fate that's holding mine
Sitting here and waiting for the deadline

Or will I realise for the first time
On the last day of my life
That I am alive?

YOUR TURN

Do you believe in destiny
Or is fate some hard bastard
Knocking on your door
In the middle of the night

Your turn to run
Your turn to hide
Your turn to choose
Your turn to try

Your turn to love
Your turn to cry
Your turn to lose
Your turn to die

TIMEBOMBS

Why do I do it to myself? Plant timebombs in my head, walk blindfolded through minefields. I can be patient as long as I'm not frustrated, I can be brave as long as I'm not scared, I can be philosophical as long as things are going my way, I can be content as long as I've got what I wanted.

ONE GOOD THING *(from the album 'Keep Walking')*

Sometimes you're patient
Sometimes you're sore
And sometimes you really think you can't take it anymore

Sometimes you're philosophical
Sometimes you're raw
But if there's one good thing about a broken heart
You can't break it anymore

You can look but don't touch desire
Your dreams are dust at dawn
And now you've got what you've been longing for
You don't want it anymore

But this time you've gone across that line
And they don't think you'll be fine
And they say you lost your mind
That you left it all behind

Cos sometimes you're lazy
And sometimes you're wrong
But if there's one good thing about a bad mistake
You won't make it anymore

But this time you've gone across that line
And they don't think you'll be fine
And they say you lost your mind
That you left it all behind
You left behind your mind

Cos sometimes we're crazy
And sometimes we're bored
But if there's one good thing about the end of time
You can't waste it anymore

EXPECTATIONS

Drown your dreams in expectation
Expect disappointment
And you will not be disappointed
Make all your fears come true
Just so you can say
You were right all along
It would all go wrong

MY CAT

My cat sleeps, staggers downstairs, eats, then waits in the hall and cries out, as if she's lost her compass, she can't remember how to find her way back up the stairs. How does time appear to a cat? Each hour like a day or a minute? What is real time? She's nearly twenty years old. That's over a hundred in cat years. So does that mean she feels like she's been alive that long? Or does she have no concept of time past, present, or future? Only binary impulses in her brain - 'hungry', 'not hungry', 'sleep', 'don't sleep', 'attention', 'leave me alone'. Does she have feelings? Yes I think so. She purrs when you comb her fur - it sounds like pleasure. She cries out - it sounds like pain. So what was her last life like? Was she a dog? Or a dolphin? Or my mother?

Mind does not need a physical body to exist. It does not need skin to imagine a boundary is there - the concept of self and other is so powerful it creates self and other even when there is no boundary. The drop in the ocean conceives of itself as a drop, not the ocean. It is still imagining itself as a drop when it is in a cloud, before righteously falling as rain - see I told you I was a drop - into a river where it runs its own race down the mountain, through the hills and valleys, back to being a drop in an ocean. Is that like the cycle of rebirth?

I HAVE BEEN DEAD

I have been dead many times
But I do not remember what it felt like
I have been alive many times
But I do not remember who I was
Every time a new beginning
Every beginning a new end

THE WISHING WELL

Put some love in my heart
And a smile on my lips
Give me poetry and sunlight
See the good in each moment
Let go of the thorn
And admire the rose
There are only so many days
Before I die
Just do it
Don't make a cage of excuses
And put your dreams inside
Like birds who cannot fly
Butterflies pinned to a board
You look at them every now and then
And sigh
"I could have, I should have, I would have"
Hands tied in fear and apathy
You never failed
Because you never tried to succeed
You were safe inside your shell
Dropped your dreams in the wishing well

GRATITUDE

Another beautiful day. Clear blue sky, sunlit frosted roofs. Strange dreams. M yesterday saying she feels frightened and angry about ageing. Frightened and angry. Those two feelings lock you up inside yourself. I know exactly what she means – or rather I've had a taste of it. So what can you do? Push back the tide? Catch the rain before it hits the ground? Or relax? You've done this countless times before. Countless. This one only counts as one. As I walk through our clean uncluttered flat this morning I am acutely aware of its impermanence. This state of living could last a year or two. And immediately that thought causes me pain. I think "I love it here", then the next minute "It must end". So why should I think that thought? To be able to see a gorgeous sunset and not want to pin it to the sky. To say how lovely that was, I'm so grateful to have seen it. Gratitude is a wonderful thing. It's hard to feel fear and anger when you're feeling grateful. So what am I grateful for?

HEAVEN IN MY HEAD

Summertime has been and gone
And colder nights are coming on
And oh god it's cold, now it's
Tipping down the avenues and
Nothing good is in the news
And oh should I stay or should I go?

But I am not the only one
To want to smile and sing a song
And oh in my soul I know
That I am not so innocent
I've sinned a lot but in the end
I know I've got to go, got to go

And I will reap what I've sown
And I will leave on my own

But I can wait for better days
And I can walk in many ways
And oh heaven's in my head
I can breathe and I can talk
And I can see and I can walk
And oh I got heaven in my head

I've been right and I've been wrong
I've felt the knife and carried on
And oh life is so priceless
I know that all these hopes and fears
Will fall away along the years
And everything is loaned, nothing's owned

And I will reap what I've sown
And I will leave on my own

But I can wait for better days
And I can walk in many ways
And oh heaven's in my head
And I can see and I can walk
And I can breathe and I can talk
And oh I got heaven in my head

Cos I'm not dead and I've been fed
And I can read about it
And I could deny or I can try
I don't need to doubt it

Cos I can breathe and I can talk
And I can see and I can walk
And oh heaven's in my head
And I can wait for better days
And I can walk in many ways
And oh I got heaven in my head

HOW I FEEL

How I feel
Is no more real
Than a rainbow
The moon in a mirror
A storm in a teacup

CHANCE

Patience is water in a river of rocks. You think they are immovable, permanent, but they are not. Slowly but surely, gently but determinedly, they are worn away.

If I was a bird, if I was a worm, if I was a snake, if I was a mountain goat, if I was any creature other than a human being, I'd have no other chance than chance.

RUSSIAN ROULETTE

Is life chance or
Is life fate or
Is life neither
But a perfect
Mathematical equation
$X + Y = Z$
Z being the outcome
You least expected
Somehow
Despite having X and Y
Y being a good word
We always ask
When things are not
Going our way
When it feels like
Chaos rather than
Order, Russian
Roulette without
The blank bullet

PAY TO BREATHE

They say a multi-billionaire
Has bought the rights to the open air
So now we have to pay to breathe
A premium rate if you're by the sea

GOOD NEWS

Imagine a life without newspapers, headlines, deadlines. No-one to sell me something I don't need, give me warnings I don't heed, make me scared and unsure, keep me always wanting more, of bombs and wars and guns and crack, however much I have I lack, keep the fires burning in the temple of greed, I have everything I want and nothing that I need. Tell me Mr Newsman:

Something good happened today
Someone had something kind to say
And the sky made a beautiful dawn
And a thousand children were born
And the birds sang the sweetest song
Someone scared became someone strong
And a stranger smiled in a crowd
I said "I love you" right out loud
And the soldiers put aside their guns
Someone's lottery ticket won
A corporation helped the poor
The bankers said we don't need more

I TURNED ON THE NEWS *(from the album 'Stranger Place')*

I turned on the news today
And they had nothing good and nothing new to say
The same old story again
They say they'd sent the soldiers out to play
At making peace a war's the only way
For peace of mind we will pray

That we're not to blame any longer
And we're not ashamed any longer
And we're not the same any longer

And all the priests and politicians prayed
But God had given up and gone away
And his Son has turned in his grave
Cos he might just as well have been saved
For all the good his sacrifice has made
For all that good advice he gave
An eye for an eye and we'll all be blinded

But we're not to blame any longer
And we're not ashamed any longer
And we're not the same any longer

Cos we're civilised, we're civilised
We wear a suit and tie
I turned on the news today
And they had nothing good and nothing new to say

We're not to blame any longer
And we're not ashamed any longer
And we're not the same any longer

So we sent the soldiers out to play
At making peace a war's the only way
The same old story again

MAD WORLD

If I'm crazy
It's cos I'm living
In a mad world

THE SONG

I'd like words to fall like flowers on this page. I would arrange them in a garland. A garland. Different words, feeling words, seeing words, words that make no sense but say exactly what I mean, words that are truthful – that "disturb the comfortable and comfort the disturbed". I would say you are not wrong, you are right, you are not bad, you are good, and you're not alone, I am here and I hear you, I will take your hand and hold it in mine and we will walk together through the valley of life and death, through sickness and old age, to the ocean's edge, and I will teach you a song that we can sing to ward off the demons and the hungry ghosts, and the words of this song you will remember in your heart through all your lifetimes, and whenever we meet again you will recognise me and smile to say how lovely to see you again, after all this time. And this song is not just our song, it's everyone's song, it's the song of our mothers, of our forefathers, of our ancestors. It's the song that says we are sentient beings, we are pure potential, we are the Buddhas, we can see as far as the stars, our minds are as wide as the sky, our hearts are as deep as the oceans. No skin can contain us, no wall can close us in, no weight can hold us down, no bricks can block us out, no fence can hem us in, for mind has no sides, no edge, no top, no bottom, no colour, no shape, no place. You can't fill space or it isn't space anymore. And you can't imprison freedom.

PART II

HOPE

Hope holds out its hand
And I grasp it in mine
I will follow its lead
See if it takes me
To a sunlit hill
Or a pit of despair
Now is not the time for choices
They've been and gone
It's time to have faith
To believe in serendipity
To walk across the moon

BELIEVER *(from the album 'Believer')*

I could be a rider, riding
I could be a runaway, a runaway
I could pray like a preacher, preaching
I could be making it easier, easy, easy, easy

Cos I try to fight the fire with fire
And I find that the only way, the only way
Was just to get higher and higher
Leaving all the loneliness, the lonely, if only

I'd seen the light of a thousand suns rising high above the sea
And I'd held the hand of a holy man if only I believed
Believer

I could be taking it easier, easy
And making it right away, the right way
And never be the lonely, if only,
And running like a rider, riding, a rider, riding

Cos I could be counted, not counting
And I could run and hide away, hide away
I try to be wanted and wanting
To keep away the loneliness, the lonely, if only

I'd seen the light of a thousand suns rising high above the sea
And I'd held the hand of a holy man if only I believed
That I've seen the light of a thousand suns rising high above the sea
And I've held the hand of a holy man if only I believed
Believer

YOU ONLY SEE

You only see darkness
Cos your eyes are closed
You only see shadows
Cos your back's to the sun

MOONCHILD

He's a moonchild. He loves truth more than fiction. He lets go of the past the way a child lets go of a balloon, with just a moment's regret before admiring its rise into the clear, big blue sky. He looks at the future with careless abandon, as if no car would ever run him down. He stands astride the present moment and laughs into the wind. Nothing can hurt him for he has no pride, nothing can take his smile away, no cloud can rain down on his bare head full of sunshine. He turns rain into rainbows, and clouds into cartwheels across the sky.

SOME OF US

Some of us are lost
Some of us have been found
Some of us are in hiding
Some of us are in the spotlight
Some of us are travelling
Some of us are homeward bound
Some of us can't sleep at night
Some of us can't stay awake
Some of us want to be on our own
Some of us don't want to be alone
Some of us have our eyes wide open
Some of us have our heads in the sand
Some of us are hopeless at leaving
Some of us just don't want to stay
Some of us can be cruel
Some of us would rather be kind
Some of us feel restless as the ocean
Some of us are rooted as a tree
Some of us are waiting for a saviour
Some of us don't want to be saved
Some of us are full of fear and loathing
Some of us are more curious than afraid
Some of us are waiting for a sign
Some of us won't wait for anything
Some of us are bruised and broken
Some of us are bold and brave
Some of us have happy memories
Some of us regret the past
Some of us say words we wished unspoken
Some of us are silent as a shell
Some of us look forward to the future
Some of us are filled with foreboding
Some of us won't go out after dark
Some of us won't come home until dawn
Some of us have our heads in the clouds

Some of us like to keep our feet on the ground
Some of us want to help but don't know how
Some of us just don't want to know
Some of us are wishing we'd run away
Some of us are wishing we'd stayed
Some of us are undecided
Some of us are certain we're right
Some of us want more than we've got
Some of us are happy with our lot
Some of us find life too hard to handle
Some of us don't want it to ever end
But all of us were born
And all of us will die
And no matter how old or how young
No matter how rich or how poor
All of us want happiness
All of us want to avoid suffering
So why should my desires
Be any more important than yours?

TROUBLE

I'd like to care a little more about you
And a little less about me
Cos looking after number one
Has brought me nothing but trouble

LOVE

Love will break your heart. So why do we do it? Are we masochists? Are we addicted? What about loving kindness – that won't break your heart. Compassion can, unless you have the armour of wisdom. Love is like a nuclear power plant – it can turn all your lights on without putting smoke into the air, but it can also destroy you and everything you've known in an instant. Too hot to handle, harder than steel, softer than down.

Love is medicine but then it kills you in the end. You love, but you lose, you learn and you choose, you burn and you bruise. Would you do it all over again? Because you will do it all over again, and again, and again. So the wheel turns, no beginning, no end, a circle not a line, and every time we have the chance to go a different way, choose the path we have not taken before. Over hills and streams, through doubts and dreams, we meet strangers who once were friends, lovers we don't recognise, magnetised this way and that, always going forward, there is no way back.

And so the wheel turns, and we learn the lessons of this life, we fall in love, we deal with strife, and stress and strain, we feel the sun, we feel the rain. And what makes us human? What makes us different from the bear who loves her cub? That is love too. She chooses not to eat her young even when she is starving. So it is not making choices. Nor is it aggression, or jealousy, or hope – doesn't the elephant dream of water as she marches for sunbaked miles to find a pool? Is it reason? What is reason? Doesn't the mouse in the lab use reason to determine where the cheese is going to be? Is it kindness? But aren't the monkeys de-fleaing each other being kind? Self-awareness? But isn't it that very concept that causes us all the trouble?

I have completely digressed. The point I was really trying to make was about how human love is at once our saving grace and our downfall. It is our salvation and our crucifixion. Maybe that's what the Christian story of Jesus is really about – love. How it can perform miracles, change the hearts and minds of men, start a huge revolution in society, and end up nailing your hands and feet to a cross where you suffocate and die, while God your father watches from a safe distance.

BIRD INSIDE A CAGE *(from the album 'Bird Inside A Cage')*

Such a wilful child, always wanted to be wild
Never thought I'd ever be a bird inside a cage
But fate has such a funny way of devastating any day
And before you know it you're in over your head
But it's love that saves us when all else has failed us
When you just can't take another day

Now I've cried countless tears, faced my biggest fears
There's nowhere to go when you can't get out of bed
If I could change that fatal moment when the chance was there
Now I'm left with fairytale castles in the air
But it's love that saves us when all else has failed us
When it's hard to see how we could carry on this way

But he calls my name like nothing's changed
And then he'll say, hey

Let me put my arms around you, never let me go
When I tell you that I love you, I want you to know
This whole damn world could fall on our heads
But I will always stay, hey

There's nothing we should take for granted
But you are all I ever wanted
And I will wear a smile when they lay me in my grave
Cos all this time we waste on foolish cares
What's the point in pride when you're running out of air
But it's love that saves us when all else has failed us
Every time you think you'll fall

You can call my name, my love won't change
It's the eternal flame

So you can dry your tears
Cos you'll defy your fears
And love is always here

AN ORDINARY LIFE

Walking the wire
An ordinary life I'll lead
And then I'll face the fire
Or a silent cemetery

CEMETERY

There's nowhere I feel more connected with the past than in a cemetery. Walking slowly down the sun-soaked path reading the names and dates and wondering how a whole life and personality can be summed up in a few simple words: "Here lies... beloved... died". Oceans of tears turned to stone. A man comes out of the trees towards me. "These places are very interesting, aren't they?" he says. "They're fantastic," I say without catching his eye, wondering if I'm safe. This response seems to satisfy him or maybe he thinks *he's* not safe because I'm crazy – cemeteries "fantastic"? Perhaps not the right word but I think they are.

Then I walk over the bridge to the supermarket past the girl on the ground begging. "No sorry," I say, not catching her eye either, then move on a few feet to the promontory where I drop some breadcrumbs for the pigeons to eat. So I would give to the birds but not to her? They won't spend it on drink and drugs is the thought in my head. A righteous thought or completely lacking in compassion? Would I do anything to help her if I thought it would do her good? In my exalted opinion?

Picked up some litter on the road. Is this a sign of trouble or good citizenship? A tidy mind or an approaching tsunami? These pages filled with lines of words and no poetry, not one lyric. What do I have to do? Talk to me – tell me. What do I have to do to turn the tap on? Is there a tap? Try? Give up? Write a little? Write a lot? I won't even try. Why won't I even try? Because I don't think I can and because I don't think I can, I can't. Simple as that. Yet I can write this stream of words perfectly easily on this page. So why not the 12 syllables of a lyric line?

Maybe my muse doesn't want to write a song, maybe she doesn't give a fuck about my career, she just wants to paint the sky and drape clouds across the sunset and have the sun sink romantically behind the large beech tree on the horizon. Maybe she wants to fill these pages with thought after thought after thought until I am done with thinking and can finally start being. Being who? Being myself. And who am I? I am human. With foibles and flaws and enough love in my heart for all the dead people in St James's Cemetery but barely any for the living in Sainsbury's. Why is that?

PHOTOGRAPHS

Her face, frozen
In photographs
Lines the walls
Of the red room
Framed by grief
She stares out
Untroubled
Happy even
Certainly not knowing
That her time
Is nearly up
That all that will remain
Of her hopes and dreams
Will be these snapshots
Capturing the moment
Before her world ended
And a world of pain began

THE MINEFIELD

I tread the minefield
In my head
If thoughts could kill
I'd be dead

THE NARRATOR

I'm always there when you start the new day
I'm always there to watch the words that you say
I make you scared and unaware so I can get my way
But I don't care about you anyway

While you're behind, I'm always one step ahead
While you unwind, I'm there to pull your thread
And I'm the one who whispers in your ear 'you're better off dead'
Yes I'm always there, the narrator in your head

I'm always there to keep you in line
I make you think that I'm your rational mind
And when you dare to think without me things could be just fine
I'm always there, there to undermine, I like to undermine

Cos I'm the drop of ink dyeing your clear water
I'm the shifting quicksand on which you falter
I'm the snake-eyed charmer lying in your bed
Yes I'm always there, the narrator in your head

I say you're missing out so that you always want more
I whisper doubts in your ear so you can never be sure
Cos that's the way I like to keep you nice and insecure
Cos I'm judging you, I like to lay down the law

I say trust me, for what I say is true
I say there's just me to tell you what to do
You know without me, you'd always get it wrong
Yes without me, you could not be so strong
You wouldn't last for long

I plague your mind when you're in your bed
As I define the life you could have led
And I remind you of the things that you should never have said
Cos I'm your commentator, the narrator in your head

RADIATION

It's often said there is a fine line between creativity and craziness. Or maybe there isn't a line at all. But it's annoying that as soon as I feel the flow of words, I also start to question the flow of feelings and start trailing myself like a policeman. I put myself under surveillance. I laughed too much, I'm too excited, I'm not sleeping straightaway, I'm writing songs – oh god no! Not writing songs surely?! Off to the doctor at once!

Mental illness is a bit like radiation: you can't physically see it but it can fuck you up completely.

LET IT LIE

Take another pill, another thrill
To feed the mental overkill
I just can't keep still inside
Cos any way and any day
A step away from yesterday
When I lost my way

Is there a better place, unfettered space
And no rat race to run me down
There's no turning round they say
If I could make a change, break the chains
And rearrange these rails I run
Could it still be done

And in another state another fate
Could I create not paper cracks
That would break my back again
Could I ever go, I've never flowed
The straight and narrow shallow stream
That would drown my dreams

Another high is another tide
I realise will always rise
And fall away from sight
Cos any way and any day
A step away from yesterday
Or so they say

But anywhere I go
Whether high or low
From my shadow I can't fly
And time won't let it
My mind won't let it
And I won't let it lie
Just let it lie

GRAVITY

Lost
In my own world
I don't see
The stars and satellites
I don't hear
The radio signals
Calling, calling
Come in Planet Earth
Are you there
Cos I'm not
I've lost my orbit
And the only thing
Keeping me hanging on
Is gravity

NEVER GIVE UP

Never give up, though the sky crashes in, thunders around your ears. Never give up, though you've got miles to go down a long lonely road. Never give up, when you've climbed so high but you're still so far from the top. Never give up, though you're feeling sad when you're supposed to be happy – your life's a beach but you're dying inside, the lights are on but you're in the dark, though the north wind throws you to the ground, though you think you can't stand up. Never give up.

STILL BEATING

It started as a whisper
I barely noticed at first
Words softly slid into my ear
Persistent, slowly surfacing
In my brain as I began to listen,
Distant at first
To the hiss and hum
Of a thread well-spun
Spinning itself into my ear
Behind the drum
Behind the door of reason
That should have stopped
The whispers growing to a roar
More and more insistent
"Worry, worry, rush and hurry
Toil and death and age and money"
Pointing, poking, screaming, shouting
"Stress, stress, panic, press
Sleep, deadline, pointless, mess"
On and on and on and on
And on and on and on and on
Until one day I stopped

And suddenly
All I could hear was silence
And the sound of my heart -
Still beating

THE LOVE YOU GAVE

I don't know how to weather this storm
I don't know how to carry on
But there is nothing out of place
And it's an ordinary day
You take my hand

I feel like I'm falling fast I said
There's no light, just darkness in my head
Darling, dry your tears you say
Cos everything will be okay
You held my hand

The love you gave told me I could make my way
Told me not to feel afraid, it'll be okay in a little while

I don't know how to stop this thing
It's like storm clouds are closing in
But see the rain has gone, you say
And it's such a lovely day, the sun is coming out

The love you gave told me I could make my way
Told me not to feel afraid, it'll be okay

So I may feel a hopeless case
But you turn around and say

The love you gave told me I could make my way
Told me not to feel afraid, told me it would be okay
It'll be okay in a little while

HOPE IS A MIRAGE

Hope is a mirage in the desert, it is a painting of water when you don't have a drop to drink, it is the word 'love' in a newspaper article when it's all you want to hear from the lips of your lover. Hope is a castle made of sand on a summer's day before the tide comes in. Hope and fear, the great double-edged sword. My hopes? In the grand scheme of things – grand being the bird's-eye view of lifetimes stretching into the distance as far as the eye can see – my life is but one step in a journey of a thousand miles, that's all. But if I make that step in the wrong direction, if I turn my head this way instead of that, the destination will change – no, not the destination, there is no destination – but the path will change forever. Instead of leading me through scented forests, it will lead me into the quagmire.

So forget hopes: they are illusions. Forget dreams: they are illusions. Forget yourself: you are an illusion. If you want to take this step in the right direction, look up, open wide your eyes and your heart, see where you really are, then look at your feet and see which way they are pointing. It's only one step, this lifetime, but it can change the course of your consciousness. Bodies grow sick, they grow old, they cause us pain. Don't pay too much heed to the body. It is mind that creates your world, every minute, every second manifesting on the big screen of your life and you are the writer, the director, the actor and the audience, watching and waiting for the credits to roll.

BORROWED TIME

Take me to the border, to no-man's land
Show me my hour-glass full of sand
And read every line written on my face
Tell me the truth of time and space
Then give me another day
To watch the sun rise and fall again
I'd say, thank you, I'm alive

For I am like an arrow shot from a bow
Down, down, down is how it goes
Leaving only my mind which has no form
It's never been dead and never will be born
And now I see the sand
Falling faster through
And I know it's going to

Cos I'm alive
So I know, yes I know I'm dying
It started right when I was born
Now I know, yes I know I'm dying
From the moment I was born
I've been living on borrowed time

Feed me to the gods but give me one more dance
I'd make my feet fly if I had the chance
Erase every hateful hope and fear
And whisper some wise words in my ear
Then give me another day
To watch the sun rise and fall again
I'd say, thank you, I'm alive

I'm alive and I know, yes I know it's getting late
But just give me one more day, another day
To be alive and I won't, no I will not waste it
I won't let it run away, run away

If I saw the border and the falling sand
I would realise, I would understand
There is no, there is no way I'll survive
I would tell you how I feel so alive

Cos I know, yes I know I'm dying
It started right when I was born
Now I know, yes I know I'm dying
From the moment I was born
So I know, yes I know I'm dying
But I don't mind cos I'll be born
I'll be living on borrowed time

SWIM

It doesn't matter how deep the water
As long as you can swim

ICEBERG

I watch the news – the latest litany of crime, corruption, death and destruction. My heart doesn't miss a beat. My eyes don't blink. My hands remain where they were. I am an iceberg, floating on an ocean that is made of the same water as me, but I am frozen solid, suspended in my delusion of separateness. I am lonely in my imagined isolation. I have more contact with my computer than any human being. I am calling from Planet Earth. Is there anyone there?

ALL THAT YOU WANTED *(from the album 'Keep Walking')*

In a dark room, alone with your head
In this silence, the words that you said
You were smiling, a smile you can't fake anymore

And timing, well time only takes
And it's writing lines on your face
And you're frightened, you don't want to face anymore

All you wanted, all you needed, all you prayed for
All that you wanted was more

Cos you thought you'd be making your name
As they taught you seek fortune and fame
But they caught you and you can't escape anymore

Cos your life is a loan you can't pay
You're providing for kids you can't save
And desiring a love you don't make anymore

And you realise the butterflies have all gone
And you feel like something's wrong

All you wanted, all you needed, all you prayed for
All that you wanted was more

So you're buying things that you crave
And denying they ever could save you
From dying, you don't want to die anymore

All you wanted, all you needed, all you waited for
All you wanted, all you needed, all you prayed for
All that you wanted was more

RUN A MILE

Sometimes the hardest thing
To do is doing nothing
To sit still when you want
To run a mile

TOMORROW

I must face the day because tomorrow always comes.
Yesterday holds no fears for me now. But the night is long
when I'm counting every hair on my head. And I'm dragged
along by thoughts like wild horses across a plain. I don't
want to go there. I want to lay my head down on a bed of
dreams. And wake in the morning with a clear head and an
easy heart.

MOLEHILL

All these fears, partly born
From the love of drama.
Would life be so much more
Ordinary, if I didn't always
Imagine the worst?
From the smallest insignificance
To the largest catastrophe
Except of course, the unimaginable,
The one thing I can be sure
Will happen. Though when,
Who knows?
The next breath or the next
Life. I am tired of living life
Scaring myself in this way.
Both ways. Wasting time alive
Worrying about dying has to be
The most pointless exercise -
The worrying part at
Any rate. Realise, but
Don't make a drama out of it.
A molehill out of a mountain

FEAR

A fish who's afraid of the sea
A bird who's afraid of heights
A blind man who's afraid of the dark
A soldier who's afraid to fight
A pilot who's afraid to fly
A diver who's afraid to jump

Failure is acceptable… fear is not.

HAPPINESS

Another day gone. Vapour trails in the sky. I missed the birds – the dusk is too far gone now. A plane, far on the horizon, leaves a silver trail behind like smoke in the clear blue air. Happiness comes in threes. You wake up one morning, you care a little less, you love a little more, being kind is more important than being cool, anger seems like a whole lot of hot air, place becomes space, time becomes opportunity not to be missed, patience is no longer perseverance, desire has become love, hope is now optimism, fear is only necessary for survival, ego has been undressed and understood for the foolish, frightened child it really is, silence has become something special, the future has become the past, the past does not matter so much anymore. Lines mean smiles and laughter, time means precious human birth, impermanence teaches us priorities and the usefulness of change, enemies become our greatest friends, fools are our teachers, wise men are beacons of light, the storm becomes a sunrise, the dark becomes dawn, I die and am born, I become old to become a child again.

BLUE

If I paint your sky blue
The sun shines for me too

STARDUST

We are stardust, the same old carbon
So why do we feel this way
All our heartaches and our troubles
Scientists can't explain

But you can see it when you close your eyes
And you can feel it where the sun kissed your face
And if heaven is freedom, then all we need is faith

Cos we are helpless in our cradle
We don't know what lies ahead
Many rivers and tall mountains
It's a long and lonely path we tread

And we've all been hypnotised by satellites
By the stars we saw
Chasing all our lives the chance of paradise
To be free once more

Cos you can see it when you close your eyes
And you can feel it where the sun kissed your face
And if heaven is freedom, then all we need is faith

That mind's an ocean, a sea with no shore
And you dreamed of an island where you've been before

Cos you can see it when you close your eyes
And you can feel it where the sun kissed your face
And if heaven is freedom, then all we need is faith

SUFFERING

When you're high, you see coincidences in everything. Is that because there *are* coincidences in everything and sane people just don't see them? Or are coincidences so blasé, there's nothing amazing in them at all? I was thinking the other night about people desperately seeking happiness, how everything we do is an attempt to make the world a more habitable place to live in, how we grasp onto things – love, looks, youth, wealth, possessions, people. We are all suffering but some infinitely more than others. It's like here in the West where we are fed and watered and sheltered, we have a hair in our eye and it's driving us crazy. While in other places people also have a hair in their eye but they don't notice it so much because they also have a knife at their throat, a block of concrete on their foot and manacles clamped around their wrists.

SONG FOR IRAQ

Once upon a time in a place somewhere
A lot of people dying with the soldiers there
You don't need to ask what they're fighting for
When there's so much money to be made from war

Congress gave, taxpayers paid
Soldiers slayed and rich men made
About a thousand billion, maybe more
Oh there's so much money to be made from war

Antiques smashed and archives spoiled
Don't worry about that, just get the oil
You want to spend cash and make some more
Well there's so much money to be made from war

No jobs, no food, no gas, no light
No law, no trust, no wrong, no right
The people who are left can't take much more
But there's so much money to be made from war

Guns and gold and God are great
Bombs and anger and blood and hate
It's love and peace that we can't afford
When there's so much money to be made from war

So men are murdered and women raped
Kids are kidnapped and found too late
But for Dick and Donald, Connie and George
There's so much money to be made from war

WORDS

Words are simply herds
Of woollen sheep to cover
Fields of fear and loathing

THE TOP

Sometimes it's more than I can bear to put one foot in front of the other. Snowstorms come, winds blow and I can't see which way I should go, but as long as it's uphill I know I'll reach the top someday. And I want to see the view from up there – the other side of the mountain – to look back and know where I'm coming from, and where it is I'm going to.

RED SEA

All these books
Full of words
Telling you
What to do
And yet when it comes
To the big decisions
The make or break
The life or death
Moments, there is nothing
But the beating
Of my heart
And the blood in my head
Pounding away
Like a red sea on a distant shore

GIVE ME THE WORDS

Give me the words so I know what to say
Give me the wisdom to know the right way
Give me the arms to hold a cold heart
Give me the hands to play my guitar

Give me the signs to show me the way
Give me the time to live, live another day
Give me a reason to walk the wire
Give me the fuel to feed this wildfire

Cos I know that there's a middle way
I can hear the wise man say
You make it, you break it too
And I know there's no such thing as fate
I choose every step I take
I make it and take it too, and so do you

Give me the heart to fill with love
Give me the eyes to see, see the birds above
Give me the ears to listen well
Give me the mind to make heaven from hell

Cos I know that there's a middle way
I can hear the wise man say
You make it, you break it too
And I know there's no such thing as fate
I choose every step I take
I make it, I make it true, create it
It's what I do and so do you

THUNDER OUT OF LIGHTNING

Letting go is harder than holding on but only if you think you'll fall and that's just my fears making thunder out of lightning again.

NORTH AND SOUTH *(from the album 'Bird Inside A Cage')*

I left when I was feeling blue
And I should have put my arms round you
But I had an angry knot inside
It was tied so tight

You know the north and south of me
Cos you've climbed my mountains, crossed my seas
And there's nothing I can hide from you
You know my dark side too

But high tide or low tide, the moon loves the sea
And through stormy weather, you still love me
You're the rain to my desert, you're the root to my tree
You're the rock in my river, you're the shore to my sea
You know the north and south of me

Cos my mind is like a maze
And I know sometimes I drive you crazy
But I get lost inside my head
Oh I should have said

I'm sorry but I ran away
And it's not that I don't want to stay
But no matter what I say or do
You know I still love you

Cos high tide or low tide, the moon loves the sea
And through stormy weather, you still love me
You're the rain to my desert, you're the root to my tree
You're the rock in my river, you're the shore to my sea

And it's you I talk to when I don't know what to say
And it's you I turn to when I've gone and lost my way

Cos you know the north and south of me
And you've climbed my mountains, crossed my seas
And there's nothing I can hide from you
You know my dark side too

And high tide or low tide, the moon loves the sea
And through stormy weather, you still love me
You're the rain to my desert, you're the root to my tree
You're the rock in my river, you're the shore to my sea
You know the north and south of me

GOOD ENOUGH

If there were words
For how I'm feeling
I would say them
"A bit low"
Isn't good enough
And not being
Good enough
Is actually
Come to think of it
The whole crux
Of the whole thing
Musician, friend,
Sister, wife
Instead of striving
To do my best
I am here doing
Nothing, feeling
Useless, like a
Spade without a handle
And since these feelings
Come and go
I am left high and dry
Just when I was
Dealing with a flood
And all of a sudden
Everything's changed
Except me, same old
Same, older, but no
Wiser as to why
This happens
Why me

CREATIVITY

I was thinking this morning that creativity is a bit like a garden. It needs some sun, it needs some rain, it needs manure (ah yes, all the shit is just manure), it needs attention and effort, it has seasons where nothing grows and other times when everything blossoms. And the seeds that grow you can't predict exactly how they'll turn out. Oh it's so easy to be philosophical when things are going well.

Is it possible to be creative without being a little crazy? Is it possible to be a little crazy without being concerned? Is it possible to be concerned without killing off the creativity? I'm taking two olanzepine tonight. Just in case. There is a fine line between being invincible on the pool table and too pissed to see the ball.

PRETENDING TO BE SANE

I'm not mad, I'm just not good at pretending to be sane.

OVER THE WATERFALL *(from the album 'Bird Inside A Cage')*

I bet you don't hear a million voices ringing in your head
I bet you don't see symbolic meaning in every word you said
And nor do I, except sometimes my reason goes
Out it flies, off to somewhere no-one knows

I lose my mind which I can't find
Cos I don't know it's missing at all
Won't you hold my hand and don't let go
Or I will fall down through the clouds
Over the waterfall

Picture this attic with a window looking at the sky
Picture some basement like a dungeon and now you ask me why
I choose the sky, I hold the whole world in my hand
Embrace the night but now I don't know who I am

I lose my mind which I can't find
Cos I don't know what's going on
Cos I'm on cloud nine and I feel fine
I've swallowed time, I've grown me some wings
And now I can fly and follow the sky
And why should I come down

I hope you don't mind if I stay under this duvet on my bed
I hope you don't mind I don't remember a single word you said
I'd like to die, end this rollercoaster ride
And so I cry, cos I can't stop this turning tide

I lose my mind, if they can't find
A cure this time, they'll take me away
In a big white van, so hold my hand
And don't let go, don't let me fall
Through the cracks in the floor
So take my hand and don't let go
Don't let me go over the waterfall

DON'T LOOK DOWN

They said don't look down
But you did and you found
You were just walking on air

THE PERFECT LINE

Coming down you're staring at the ground. Going up you're looking at the sky. The view is great up there. Life carries on regardless. There is no real world. Medication makes illusory boundaries just as mind makes illusory wings. Where does the illusion stop and the reality begin? A dream within a dream within a dream, like those infinity mirrors. Infinity: no end, no beginning, a circle, not a line. Old ideas, old thoughts, old feelings surface like seaweed at low tide – ugly, compelling you not to get in the water but stand on the hard rock gazing at the perfect line of a horizon you cannot reach because it is a mirage, it doesn't exist: the dissecting sea and sky is actually a disappearing curve.

ECLIPSE

So rare the moon
Takes centre-stage
During the day
The sun for once
Behind
Like a shy child
And we can all remember
Where we were
The last time
This happened
And so I'm thinking of you
And how far away
The present moment is
From that day on the hill
As far away
As the moon from me

ROUND THE BEND

Something amazing is just round the corner but you've got to go round the bend to see it.

TONGLEN

So I think I'm feeling better and we go to London. Sitting on the tube, anxiety and disorientation start to seep into my eyes, and I feel trapped in a looking glass, in a goldfish bowl, with normal people in a big city sitting so close to me, strangers in a tunnel and I think I'm going to cry so I stare at the strange blood-flecked floor and feel the blood rush to my cheeks and I count my breaths but that makes it worse and I think of the Lama but the anxiety just grows then I think "Let all the anxiety everyone else is feeling come into me" and suddenly it stops. Fades away. The arrows turn into flowers and I get out at Oxford Circus and walk down the street, head held high.

IF I COULD SEE YOU *(from the album 'Stranger Place')*

I met a man with a hand on his face
I said what hell are you hiding from
And he said I just can't stand this sense of space
And my hand is my hiding place
I said if I could see you the way you see yourself
I wouldn't recognise you

I met a woman, she had eyes that burned
I said what light are you looking for
And she said I blinked before and I missed my turn
And I think it's all too late to learn
And I said if I could see you the way you see yourself
I wouldn't recognise you

I wouldn't recognise you the way you see yourself
I don't recognise you the way you see yourself

I met a girl with a curling smile on her face
I said for what good reason are you so happy
She said I have no reason, just a feeling inside
Cos right here and right now I'm pleased to be alive
I said if I could see you the way you see yourself
I wouldn't recognise you

I wouldn't recognise you the way you see yourself
I don't recognise you the way you see yourself

CLOUDS

I don't mind clouds
They cool the sunburnt sky

THE BLACK DOG

The black dog walked me down to the valley of despair, but I left him there, and climbed high to the hilltop, and admired the view, and looked at the horizon where the sun was bending down to kiss the earth and I looked down at the valley below and saw that it was enveloped in a gentle silver mist, so delicate, so transient, I could have scooped it up in my hand, so that all the people below could see that the sky doesn't stop at the clouds – all the time, the sun has been shining.

THE HITCHHIKER

Life has so many
Twists and turns
You never know
What's going to happen
Until you career
Round the corner
And find fate
Waiting for you
Like that hitchhiker
You picked up
The other day
With his sign saying
Glasgow when you were going
To Edinburgh

HOW CAN I BE ANGRY

How can I be angry
with the tide for turning,
with the fire for burning?

THE PRESENT MOMENT

What's the point in dreaming of a materialistic future? The future doesn't exist and any material objects I'll have to leave behind when I die. Even grasping after the songs – what does it matter? In 50 years no-one will have heard of my songs, they'll be gone like flowers in the spring, snow in the winter. To be calm and relaxed – a much wiser idea. Everything changes, everything is changing, there are no guarantees. My body is a temporary hostel, and even that is starting to decay. Thinking about the countless lives that have come before this one and the countless lives that will follow makes me less attached to this one. Yet the opportunity is there in this life, that maybe wasn't there in any of the others. Think about it, really think about it. What will ambition do for me when I die, except make me regret? What will wealth do for me, except pay for a nice coffin? What will talent do for me? Nothing. I'm going to die and I will definitely experience it. There's no getting out of it. I don't know how and I don't know when. The only two certain things are that I am going to die, and that I am alive now. The present moment is all there is in all existence.

THE CROSSROADS

I lay my head back
And gaze up at the stars
They speak of history
And of the space there where they are
The light that's travelling
Through time toward my eye
Is a silver thread unravelling
All the space between it and I
In the pitch black sky

I lie in my bed
And in my head pass the sleepless time
And the questions slide in softly
Through the stained steel cage of my mind
And there they lie, undermining me
For no sane answers I can find
When I'm standing once again
At the crossroads asking just one more time
Which way is mine?

Cos I don't know where I'm going to
Or even where I'm coming from
There's no signpost at this crossroads
To tell me which way is the one
But I'll forget all these thoughts and feelings
And even the deeds I've done
And I'll regret all those wonderful things
I could and should have done
When I was young

If I take that road
There could be a bend somewhere
But for all I know it could lead me
To a dead end of despair

I could be there fulfilled
And wondering why I was oh so full of fear
Or I could be here sat still
And wondering what did happen to the years
And wishing I had dared

How shall I leave my mark
Or move a memory
I'll be a whisper in the dark
Or a cry lost on the sighing breeze
How can I make my mark
And take a part in history
When I don't know at this crossroads
Which road follows my destiny
It's a mystery to me

Cos I don't know where I'm going to
Or even where I'm coming from
There's no signpost at this crossroads
To tell me which way is the one
But I'll forget all these thoughts and feelings
And even the deeds I've done
And I'll regret all those wonderful things
I could and should have done
When I was young

Cos if I take this road
Well I could come to there
But if I take that road
Well then who knows where I'll be
In a hole or in history?

THE LAST THING

Do you think that dying is the last thing that will happen to you?

WISHING AND WANTING

I've had enough of hoping, banging my head against the same old brick wall. The bricks don't dissolve, my head just hurts more. What about giving up, climbing up to see the view from up high, more of you and less of I? Trying to look after number one hasn't got me anywhere, hasn't made me happy, so how about I spend some time trying to make you happy instead? Maybe I could make you happy and that would make me happy. It wouldn't be a hook to hang my hopes on, dangling in the wind, wishing and wanting, wishing and wanting, as the days stream by like seagulls in the sky, ducking and diving and disappearing into the blue.

CHOICES

All these choices we make
A million a day
Like the little turns
On a steering wheel
Nudging us this way or that
Or turning us round completely
Did we ever know
Where we were heading
Before we made that
Final choice
That brought us to a
Dead-end, that no matter
Which way we turned,
Was always going to
End us there?

LOST

You've never been so lost
But still you just won't ask the way
But you just won't ask and won't stop
And pride is not the price you pay

Cos you've never been so down
And now the only way is up
But you're just worn out, there's no doubt
An ocean couldn't fill your cup

You shut that door that could have opened
In the brick wall that you'd built inside your head

But you're the writer of every word
That locked you up and threw away the key
And you can't read the writing on the wall
Even though you wrote it all and you built the wall

You've been so lost so long
Cos you never thought you'd find your way
You thought there was nothing to be done
But you could have prayed

Instead you built a brickwalled barricade
Of angry words and wishes in your head

But you're the writer of every word
That locked you up and threw away the key
And you can't read the writing on the wall
Even though you wrote it all and you built the wall

The sky was never angry
You never were to blame
You never were fated just fateful
Your fatal mistake

You thought that every dream would rust and die
And every fear would come alive
And every time, time was wrong
And you'd been right all along the way

But you're the writer of every word
That locked you up and threw away the key
And you can't read the writing on the wall
Even though you wrote it all and you built the wall

EVERY DREAM

Every dream has its
Doubt
Like a sundial and its
Shadow
Turning, turning

THE CAPTAIN

I think I'm the captain of this ship. But I don't even know which ocean I'm sailing on, let alone which way the wind is blowing and if I'll ever find my way back to the shore.

TEMPORARYNESS

What is the human condition other than suffering and the transcendence of suffering? Yes achievement is transitory, but why should that be a bad thing? I don't necessarily want the sunset to last forever – I want to go to bed. If you keep grasping, clutching onto time and space, sure that will hurt, but what if you didn't grasp, just practised gratitude? I am grateful for my temporary marriage, I am grateful for my temporary good fortune, I am grateful for my temporary life. But I don't feel very grateful, I feel anxious at the word 'temporary' – so I'm grasping, so the temporaryness, inevitably, will cause me sorrow and pain. But what if out of that sorrow and pain comes compassion and creativity, a song that will slide into the mind of the listener and grow like the flowers on the hillside?

IMPERMANENCE

Do I want the sea made out of concrete,
The sky pinned up,
Clouds nailed down,
The leaves glued to the trees?

LET IT GO

When the birds head for the horizon
And the clouds are turning grey
When the light of day is fading
Let it go

When your eyes are lined with laughter
And your hair is going grey
When your youth is far behind you
Let it go

And fly home safely
When sleep calls your name
And when your mind is tired of thinking
Let it go, let it go

When the north wind starts blowing
And the nights are drawing in
When you see that summer's over
Let it go

When your heart is full of anger
And it's harsh words that you say
When your love has turned bitter
Let it go

And fly home safely
When sleep calls your name
And when your dream fades as you're waking
Let it go, let it go

When the crimson tide is ebbing
And the twilight fades to black
When your life is finally ending
Let it go

DO IT

Would I rather write a soulless pop song that was a hit or a beautiful song that deeply affected a few people? Skin deep, or from the heart? Why spend all this time analysing it and less time doing it! The wisdom of the sages seems to say, "Do it". If your practice isn't perfect, do it. If you want to climb a mountain, do it. If you want to learn a craft, do it. If you want to make the most of life, do it.

I can hear the wind. And the birds singing, and the ticking of the clock, sounds steeped in silence, and in a corner of the room a friendly ghost sits watching me, waiting for the penny to drop, wanting to tell me what my heart already knows: that creativity is an ocean, and I am standing on the shore, watching the tides come and go, wishing I could swim, when all I have to do is dive in.

A ROSE IS NOTHING *(from the album 'Bird Inside A Cage')*

A rose is nothing
Without its thorn
And there's no calm like it
In the eye of a storm

And love is nothing
When you lie
I can see those secrets
In your eyes

Life is nothing
But an endless stream
Of strange illusions
A waking dream

And hope is nothing
Without its fears
You could fill up an ocean
With all these tears

A heart is nothing
Without its beat
You can ride wild horses
In your sleep

And fire is nothing
Without its flame
You can have your reasons
But don't explain

Under this willow tree
There's no love for me

WHEN I DIE

When I die
Will I realise
That all this time
I've been dreaming
And I just woke up?

THE HOLE

Funny how someone can be such a huge part of your life and then be cut out, and gradually things grow around the hole until it disappears into the undergrowth and you'd hardly know it was there until something triggers a memory and you stumble on the opening and see the hole is still there but it's much smaller than you remember – that huge chasm of emptiness when he had gone – the chasm is hidden underground now, like a cave, and the entrance is just an unassuming hole, not much bigger than a passing thought, where you step inside for a moment, then back out into the open air again, back into your new forest of heather and gorse, where wildflowers grow, and life goes on.

MEMORY *(from the album 'A Bit Of Blue')*

Looking at a photograph
Of a faded frozen face I thought I knew
And I don't know the place or time,
The feelings but a trace defined by you

The sun caught your shadow stalking
Sees you walk across the moon
And in my mind you left behind
A footprint like the sign upon the rune

And a bright blue flame remains

Creatures cry when you catch their eye
In your hand, and they don't understand
Cos they were only laughing at the path
That you were tracking in the sand

With a shadow for a footstep
And a curtain for a wall
You're a whisper in a conversation
Cos no-one heard you call

And just a bright blue flame remains
And remembers like the embers of the forest
Where the burning trees smell of memory

Maybe I'm not on your mind
I never stopped to ask, you thought I knew
And I don't know what you believe
But you can't see the dark side of the moon
And I can't read the sign upon the rune

And a bright blue flame remains
And remembers like the embers of the forest
Where the burning trees smell of memory

MARRIAGE

Marriage begins with romance
And ends with death
Or a divorce
Oh happy thoughts

ALBATROSS

I feel lost. There are too many clothes in the cupboard. Too many clothes in the drawer. There is dirt everywhere, cracks, dust, chips, and I don't know where to go or what to do tomorrow because my mind is not my own and I need to stay very still and not make a fool of this foolish heart with its beat that has hope-fear-hope-fear-hope-fear like a drum in my ear.

One day the beat will stop and I'll hear a silence where all of a sudden things will make sense and I'll realise I don't need hope, I don't need fear, there is no 'I' to need these things. What does it matter how I look when there's no-one to see me? I can feel anything and you would never know. My dreams are purple and green and I'm trying to get somewhere and it comes close then far, close then far, like trying to leave the house with this or that, this or that.

And I'm not as crazy as I sound, I'm just leaning over the cliff edge, wanting to see what's down there. I won't fall because I'm too full of fear to let my fingers go, too full of hope to launch myself into the air like an oversized albatross, to the surprise of the wheeling seagulls and the waiting waves below.

SUICIDE

When all you want to do is die
Put the kettle on
And make a cup of tea
You can always pour
The boiling water over your hand
To give you a taste
Of the hell that awaits
After you take all those pills
Or just make you realise
The pain you were in
Inside your head
Wasn't so bad after all

WRONG TURN

Hard to know whether you've taken a wrong turn or you just can't see over the hill yet.

PART III

MANDALA

Yesterday I felt like I was in a dark ocean looking up at the surface waves tossing and turning while I hung lifeless in this strange half-light suspension, breathing salt water and going down like a suicidal diver who has left his air canister behind.

One breath can take you down a long way. We spend every waking moment constructing the world around us, making it real, like a giant sand mandala – here I am at one corner making tiny coloured patterns, a whole universe of sand that seems real to me until the wind blows and it's gone in an instant.

So on a more positive note that means all the fears and anxieties are also sand, illusions of castles and dungeons. All in my head. Disconnect. So connect. You know the drill, you know how this goes. And comes, and goes. You can walk in the dark but it helps to have a torch.

I rearrange my thoughts like chess pieces on a board – they line up, a putative army, waiting for me to make the first move. I am playing both sides of course. I am also deciding the rules as I go along. So I am both winner and loser, player and opponent. I am opposite myself, an observer, and also the observed. I am the navel and the gazer.

SENSE AND REASON

You see a blanket
I see a hole
You see sense and reason
And I see my soul
Oh you see the future
I see it past
You can let it go
But I don't see it last no

I'd like to have your eyes
Being clever's not so good as being wise

But stars are only seen
Cos of the blackness in between
I'm only working this out
And shadows are only made
Cos of the sunshine and the shade
If I can dream I can doubt

I wish that I could be wise
I'd like to see right through your eyes

But you pass the hours
While I waste time
Holding onto every moment
Like it's mine
And you see the flowers
I pull out weeds
But love is in your eyes
When you look at me

WIDE AS THE SKY

I'd like my mind to be
Wide as the sky
Blue no matter what shit
Is going on beneath it

BONVILS

They finished the field. Kettle on. Keyboard and guitar unpacked. Hazy day. Grass bobbing and bowing to the wind. Butterflies. Crows picking the shaven field. The clock ticks. I sit at the big table by the open glass doors. What a beautiful day to be alive. While I am alive, there is possibility, where there is possibility there is chance, where there is chance there is luck, where there is luck there is serendipity, where there is serendipity there is gratitude, where there is gratitude, there is love. So all I need is to love a little more, and everything else will follow.

The sun sinks slow like she's reluctant to end the day.

LIGHTHOUSE MAN *(from the album 'Believer')*

You are the star burning bright in my sky
You're the light on the wall where there's no light at all

And you're the guiding hand
You're the lighthouse man
To show me the way
And you're the firelight
You're the star at night
The sun in my day

Too many lives I've been riding these waves
And I reach for the shore but I keep going astray

I need a lighthouse man
Or a guiding hand
To show me the way
And you're the firelight
You're the star at night
The sun in my day

Each faint horizon I reach but in vain
After each sunny day comes a week in the rain

But you're the firelight
You're the star at night
The sun in my day
And you're the guiding hand
You're the lighthouse man
To show me the way

Please turn that light on, that light on
The sun in my day
Turn that light on, that light on
Show me the way

161

TRAIN

Here's this feeling again
With thoughts attached
Like the engine of a train
Dragging me into yet another
Tunnel. I could slam on
The brakes, say I'm getting off
Not even wait for the
Next station but jump down
Onto the track and
Start running, as fast as I can
Like a bat out of hell

ONE THOUGHT

It takes just one thought to change my world.

STILL BREATHING

I test the water, wary, like there's a crocodile lurking beneath the surface. But this is what I love, this is who I am, this is what I do. Got this quavers idea I really like but I'm struggling with a verse. It'll come - go away, come back again. There's a blue sky behind my window. Maybe I'm struggling because it's the wrong verse. I always seem to have a square peg for a round hole. No, not always. Maybe it's the right verse, I just don't recognise it. Today is Thursday again. Last week Thursday was a rock-bottom day. But here I am, still breathing.

START OVER AGAIN *(from the album 'Believer')*

Caught in the muddy waters, falling down
If I could breathe, then I would drown
I'm fifteen, I feel older than God
I got dreams and a hole in my heart

And he said go slow, be kind, be wise
Start over again

Out of the muddy waters, I come round
I said I'm off to London town
My love is strong, the years roll by
But now it's gone in the blink of an eye

And he said go slow, you need time, be wise
Start over again

Thrown in the muddy waters, I come down
And you were waiting there on the ground
And then you put your hand in mine
You put your heart on the line

And you said we'll go slow, you need time, be mine
And start over again

So pour on the muddy waters, I won't drown
I'll be walking a hilltop town
And I will make the most of time
And someday to a child of mine

Well I'll say go slow, be kind, be wise
Start over again

TICK-TOCK

How many more times
Will my heart beat
Until it stops
Like the clock ticking
Tick-tock
A timebomb waiting
To explode
To blow me into the
Next life
Or show me the
Next dream on this
Never-ending cinema screen

PAINTING BLACK

How can you make yourself happy by talking about your unhappiness? Isn't that like trying to paint white by painting black?

REASONS FOR LIVING

I had the thought yesterday that I should focus more on how I behave than how I feel. How you behave can change how you feel - positive action and interaction. Smiling at someone when you're feeling shit makes you feel better. But in the end I just sometimes want to walk out of my life. And the sky doesn't care, it stays blue. My eyes dry eventually. My legs keep walking. I think of reasons for living.

SHE KNOWS *(from the album 'Keep Walking')*

She knows what's coming
And it's not gonna be the brightest day
And she knows what's round the corner
And it's not gonna stop until it's over

And I wish I had the words to take it all away
I wish I had the heart to be broken
I wish I had a smile that could save her in a while
But I can bow my head and I can pray
Eyes wide open, wide open, wide open

She knows what's coming
You love and you leave your heart wide open
And she knows the story's ending
And happily ever after is never spoken

And I wish I had the words to take it all away
I wish I had the heart to be broken
I wish I had a smile that could save her in a while
But I can bow my head and I can pray
Eyes wide open, wide open, wide open

THREADS

One or two threads
At first
Not so as you'd notice
Then a frayed edge
Visible, frustrating
Then quite suddenly
At some unforeseen moment
The whole thing unravels
And I'm confronted
By what I really am -
Threads

RAINBOW

Winspit, Isle of Purbeck. Standing on the cliff edge in the pouring rain, head bowed in utter despair, I prayed to all the Buddhas and Bodhisattvas to fill my heart with love and confidence. Looked up a moment later to see a huge rainbow over the horizon, rising out of the sea. So bright, so clear, like an answer.

STAND STILL

I need to take time
To unwind the tangled threads of thought in mind
To abate the swirling wordstorm in my head
As I lie sleepless in my bed
Press pause before I play away my hand and overkill
I need to stand still

But I've got to calm down
And stop rushing around, going out as I'm coming in
Always ending up with another drink in hand
And crashing out where at last I land
Like my feet are flying off the ground
Running far too fast down a steeper hill

So I need to stand still
And empty out my mind
And fill my ears with the silence on the hill
I need to see that perfect line and the open sky behind
Until I can find the will inside to carry on

I need to slow down
Blow away the dust that's drowning out the sound
Of the words I couldn't find to express
What's stressing out my mind
As I feel hypnotised by a hundred thoughts
And feelings flying round like a watermill

I need to stand still and watch that sunlit sky above my head
And hear the silence lying in my bed
Instead a hundred voices are crying out my name
I've got to get away before they drive my mind insane

I'll plan a change
And drain the dam that's strained to bursting in my brain
I'll rearrange my trials and tribulations

The people, places and obligations
Distil my mind and purify the silt before it overspills
So I need to stand still

But I need some time
To try and redefine, realign my point of view
Instead of pouring myself yet another whiskey
I write another list of things to do
While yet another door open closes
And I find I missed my cue, I lose the will

I need to stand still and watch that sunlit sky above my head
And hear the silence lying in my bed
Instead a hundred voices are crying out my name
I've got to get away before they drive my mind insane

I said I need some space
To take a break from all the feelings in my face
I'd separate my head and heavy heart
It's another time to make another start
I could climb back on the treadmill just in time
If only I could find the will to stand still

I need to stand still, I need to stand still
I need to stand still

I need to stand still and watch that sunlit sky above my head
And hear the silence lying in my bed
Instead a hundred voices are crying out my name
I've got to get away before they drive my mind insane

I need to stand still
And empty out my mind
And fill my ears with the silence on the hill
I need to see that perfect line and the open sky behind
Until I can find the will, until I can find the will inside
To carry on

WASHING MACHINE

I am curled up in my own washing machine, spinning round and round but never getting clean.

LEAVES

So I've got this new song that I'm scared I won't write words for, but I'm listening and thinking what's the point? All these songs I love, songs from my heart, aren't going to make this album so they're just debris. Why make more debris when there's nowhere to put it? What's the point? But then I must remember that songs are just leaves on a tree and what a tree does to keep living is grow leaves, grow leaves and then let them go, grow seeds then let them go, scattered to the winds, or buried in the earth below.

AIR

What to do
When you're frightened
Of the future
And you have no control
Not even the semblance
To change things
To move them this way
Or that
Not for want of wishing
So all you are left with
Is hope and that
Feels like dangling on
The end of a very long rope
And all that is below
You is air

HIGH HOPES

From high hopes it's a long way down.

SOLITAIRE

Solitaire
Where the sea runs wild
On the ancient isle
You'll find me solitaire

I'll be there
Where the seagulls fly
You can hear their cry
Echoing in the air

When I'm lost and down
And I need some time
On my own to settle all the feelings
Overwhelming me

Solitaire
On the old stone seat
In the fields of wheat and barley
I'll be there

If you came down the winding road
You'll soon see the headland over there
Walk towards the silver sea
And you will find me there

Solitaire
With the wild white waves
And the cliffs and caves
I find my solitaire

By the sea
When the north wind blows
And my heart is overwrought
And ill at ease

When my life feels wrong
And I can't be strong
Get away from all the crowd of things
That just won't let me be

Solitaire
When the leaves turn brown
When I'm feeling down
I need my solitaire

If you came down the winding road
You'd soon see the headland over there
Walk towards the silver sea
And you will stop and stare
You will find me there

NOT ALONE

It occurred to me this morning that if life is suffering then pretty much everybody is suffering in one way or another all the time. So why should I be any different? This makes me feel weirdly better - not a very charitable thought but the truth. I am not alone, I am just normal.

SO HOW DO I FEEL?

Like I'm a wheel that won't turn
A fire that won't burn
A sea with no shore
A key with no door
A bread that won't rise
A shoe the wrong size
A brick with no wall
A bat with no ball
A wave that won't break
A dish you can't make
A grass that won't grow
A seed you can't sow
A train with no rail
A ship with no sail
A knife that can't cut
A case that won't shut
A lamp you can't light
A pen that won't write
A sun that can't shine
A verse that won't rhyme
A dog that can't bark
A car that won't start
A duck that can't dive
A plant that won't thrive
A song you can't sing
A bell that won't ring
A shark that can't bite
A day with no night

SOMEBODY *(from the album 'Stranger Place')*

If you're not a money-maker
Then you're never gonna be somebody
And if you're not a mover or a shaker
You're a loser and a fake nobody

You're no ordinary sinner
You'd have the devil round for dinner
If you thought you had a soul to sell
Hey hey, and he'd agree
That heaven's all economy
You need a first-class ticket to hell
To be somebody

Cos you're a fly high-roller
You're no low-down dirty doler
Like the beggar never catching your eye
You're too high from all the snow
Down the slopes and up your nose
You've got the strut and sniff that says
Well I'm somebody

Somebody who knows the size
Of a social backside
And has a tongue that's long enough to lick
Nobody would ever know
From the length of your nose
Your latest phone is the size of your

You're not a pawn in a pocket
Or a number on a docket
If you want it then you've got it to show
Nobody would ever guess
That there's a bra around your chest
Under the suit they made in Savile Row
Oh no, nobody

If the papers keep a diary
Of your stay inside The Priory
You know you've hit the top of the list
Hey, hey, you've got a cyst
And it's the size of Satan's fist
But you can't stop
Cos you won't be missed
When you're nobody

If you're not a money-maker
Then you're never gonna be somebody
And if you're not a mover or a shaker
You're a loser and a fake nobody

THINKING OF ME

I spent all my life
Wondering
What others were
Thinking of me
And I never realised
They weren't
Thinking of me
At all

IF I WAS WISE

If I was wise would I be fearful, or fearless? Maybe anxiety is good – better to be mindful than mindless, careful than careless.

WOKE UP *(from the album 'Believer')*

I woke up this morning, all the trees were gone
A concrete jungle left outside, oh no
They said on the radio, the seas were warm
And all the fish had gone and died, oh no

So what do we do now?

I woke up this morning all our water's gone
But now the ocean's at my door, oh no
They said on the radio a storm would come
And wash away my neighbourhood, oh no

So what do we do now?

I woke up this morning all the birds were gone
And politicians act alarmed, oh no
They said on the radio we'll wait and see
The economy cannot be harmed, oh no

*But can you see
Do you believe it now?*

A NEW PLANET PLEASE

Can we have a new planet please?
With birds and bees
And lots of fish in a deep blue sea
Can we have a blue sky
And a red earth
And a yellow sun
To light it all
Can we have mountains high
And valleys low
And sand and shingles,
Soil and snow
Can we have green and golden
Fields of wheat
And lots of things
That we can eat
Can we have dusk
To take us into night
And dawn to wake us
To the light
Can we have jungles and forests
Full of life
And trees and flowers
For the wife
Can we have a new planet please
Cos this one's passed its sell-by-date
We've taken everything we want
The paintwork's scratched
The trimmings gone
It's old and battered
And too broke to fix
A write-off you could call it
The forests are gone
The sun is burning
The seas are warming
The fish are dying

The icebergs are melting
The sky is falling
For the sake of our economy
Can we have a new planet please
That's bigger, better
More cost-effective
Less of a hassle
More of a breeze
Where money really does grow on trees

CLIMATE CHANGE

All the talk is of climate change
But it doesn't look like
We're going to
Change
Much except our
Climate

Will nations be more united
When the United Nations
Has to move its headquarters
To higher ground?

PLANET EARTH

All the clouds up in the sky
They don't care what we do
All the stars and satellites
You wouldn't know if they knew
It's all true

And when you know that
There's no going back

For a long time
The earth was life for all
And even I know
There won't be life at all
In the end

But all the while we're in denial
Will it only be proved
When all the seething oceans rise
And not a thing we can do

You see the future is a hole
That we're falling down

For a long time
The earth was life for all
And even I know
There won't be life at all
In the end

Burnt trees and bitter skies
A whole world made of glue
All the birds and butterflies
Even they know it's true

When there is nothing but a hole
And we're falling down
There'll be time to wish we'd been wise
Wish that we'd saved our planet earth
When we had the chance

For a long time
The earth was life for all
And even I know
There won't be life at all
Yes you and I know
There won't be life at all
In the end

OUT OF THE DARKNESS

Something will come. Something out of the darkness, a tiny light like the evening star will appear, and at that moment you will know there is space beyond the sky, from where anything could come, out of the darkness.

FOR FREE *(from the album 'A Bit Of Blue')*

The ancient rivers run dry
There's not enough space in the sky
But no-one owns the birds in the trees
They fly for free

I've got a thousand friends I never see
I can talk to anyone I please
But it's like some social disease
No friends know me

And it's a world of traders and thieves
Everything I want is what I need
And the wily salesman agrees
He smiles for free

But I know there's something sacred
In all the living things I see, yeah yeah
And I know that it's a wonderful world
And yes it's all for free

So I'm a little dazed and confused
There's a billion stars I could choose
And you can buy the moon if you please
But she'll shine for free

But when a man of fortune is paid
For every bomb and bullet that's made
Who would turn a war into peace
When true love is for free

But I know there's something sacred
In all the living things I see, yeah yeah
And I know that it's a wonderful world
And yes it's all for free

WHEN I'M OLD

Will I cry when I'm old
Will I wish that I'd been bold
If I'd been brave, if I had dared
If I'd made castles in the air
But no I sit here paralysed
Wondering whether I'll be wise
When I'm old

THIS PATH I TREAD

This path I tread is a path well worn
I'd been dead long before I was born

THE HABIT OF HAPPINESS

The Lama said enjoy what you do. Everything you do. So that includes today and tomorrow, not waiting for some utopia to materialise in the future that never will because I'm not in the habit of happiness.

TREES IN THE MIST

My troubles line up
Like infantry
Shoot down the first row
And the relief lasts
A nanosecond
As the second row appears
What to do
When you're facing
An army
Sit down on the ground
Say "Do with me what you will
I will not be moved"
Would they disappear
Like trees in the mist
There but not there
All in my mind?

STONE AND SKY *(from the album 'A Bit Of Blue')*

She's alone in a cemetery
Skulls and bones underneath her feet
Used to be alive
Used to be

People just like you and me
Loving, living on these city streets
And now here they lie
Under stone and sky

She knows there's a remedy
For hungry ghosts in a cemetery
She's afraid of life
She's afraid to die

Can you feel her stare when no-one's there
The black crows caw overhead
Will you take her hand and lay her down
Back in her warm earthy bed

As the clouds go by
Under stone and sky

She's alone in a cemetery
Standing under the willow tree
Can you read the stone
Says she died long ago

Can you feel her stare when no-one's there
The black crows caw overhead
Will you take her hand and lay her down
Back in her warm earthy bed

As the clouds go by
Under stone and sky

HUMAN

Reading about hungry ghosts and thinking about my insatiable desires - avarice. The longing to possess. Money, fame, praise, pleasure. Resentful of others who have it. How to overcome this? How to sit still and feel contentment? Gratitude is the antidote? Realising the uselessness of these things? Will they help me when I die? All that you wanted was more. More. And what do I have? More than most people could ever dream of, so now I indulge in guilt, and then self-anger, then self-pity. What a waste of a mind, of a precious human birth. What can I do with this mind, this life, this time? I sit still on my cushion while a storm rages in my head. Well actually, to be a tad less melodramatic, I feel intense frustration generated by my negative thoughts. Desire burns never-ending fuel. Desire to be better, to have more, to succeed. What does that mean? A three-bedroom house? A review in The Guardian? I could laugh at myself, that would be a good first step. All this attention does no good at all. I am, after all, only human. Flawed, confused, self-centred. Human. Why do you think it takes so much practice, the perfections? Because I've been this way for eons. And now I'm trying to change. Unlike the well-worn track to the lower realms of Samsara, it's a hard path to walk down. But I'm not giving up now.

THE GREAT PRETENDER

Fill me with emptiness
Drain every drop of this
Bad bad blood
Running through my veins
Bile in my brain
I try to stop it
From vomiting
Out my mouth
For all to see
Oh I care
What they think of me
I run my mind down
A serrated edge
Little cuts
Little tears
Blood drips
From paper cuts
Papering over cracks
Like canyons in my mind
But I'm still the Great Pretender
I sit on my throne
With the sea at my feet
And the gulls wheeling
High overhead
My feet are wet
My head is high
The gulls have plucked
Out both my eyes
But still I see
A whole universe
And it's all about me
The actors leave the stage
As I take my endless bow
But the hall is empty
There is no-one here
Not even me

THE GIVING BLUES

I gave him water
He wanted wine
I gave him space
He wanted time

I gave him a knife
He wanted a spoon
I gave him the sun
But he wanted the moon

I gave him silence
He wanted sound
I gave him a sceptre
He wanted a crown

I gave him a table
He wanted a chair
I gave him a circle
He wanted a square

I gave him wood
He wanted stone
I gave him skin
But he wanted bone

I gave him a necklace
He wanted a ring
I gave him summer
He wanted the spring

I gave him cotton
He wanted silk
I gave him butter
He wanted milk

I gave him a hedge
He wanted a tree
I gave him a river
But he wanted the sea

I gave him yellow
He wanted maroon
I gave him July
He wanted June

I gave him a plate
He wanted a bowl
I gave him my heart
But he wanted my soul

THE HARD WAY

Unfortunately patience you can only learn the hard way.

EMPTINESS

Reading the Dalai Lama's book, a lecture on emptiness. Find it hard to get my head around. Then reading Shamar Rinpoche's book talking about emptiness as a magic show - where the magician sees the appearance of something, as does the audience, but only he knows it's an illusion. But why is suffering an illusion? Surely that's 'real' - you feel pain, discomfort. 'All phenomena are devoid of a self'. I need to read it all again. I wish I could see clearly. There's a difference between knowing a blue sky is up there behind the clouds and actually seeing it. Oh to be a Buddha, to see beyond all this. What would I do then?

STILLNESS

Time is a menace
Stillness a crime
What can you do
To fill up your mind

Read a paper
Play with your phone
Check your appearance
Don't be alone

Turn on the TV
Go to the shops
Bite your nails
Look at your watch

Put on your make-up
Change your clothes
Check in the mirror
Scratch your nose

Make some tea
Watch a show
Talk to a friend
Turn on the radio

Type an email
Send a text
Then decide
What to do next

Pluck your eyebrows
Play with your hair
Make a hot drink
Sit in a chair

Cross your legs
Open a book
Open the fridge
Decide what to cook

Turn on the news
Take off your clothes
Get onto ebay
Get off the phone

Turn off the lights
Get into bed
Face the silence
And space in your head

BRAVE NEW WORLD *(from the album 'Believer')*

Educated, emancipated, motivated, liberated, medicated
Brave new world
Estimated, investigated, calculated, complicated, isolated
Brave new world

You shouldn't walk that wall, you shouldn't try to call
You shouldn't cry at all, and you shouldn't, you shouldn't fall
You shouldn't walk that way, you shouldn't talk that way
You shouldn't try to say, in a brave new world

Can I take my time, can I make up my mind
Can I bend the line, can I ever be a friend of mine
And can I seek my goal, can I keep control
Can I break the mould without breaking my soul

Oh no you shouldn't, no you shouldn't talk that way
And you shouldn't, no you shouldn't feel this way, it ain't okay
And you couldn't, no you couldn't walk that way
Cos it wouldn't, no it wouldn't be ok, oh no

I wouldn't walk that wall, I wouldn't try to call
I wouldn't cry at all, and I wouldn't, I wouldn't fall
I wouldn't walk that way, I wouldn't talk that way
I wouldn't try to say, in a brave new world

Innovated, rehabilitated, integrated, insulated, suffocated
Brave new world
Dissipated, concentrated, radiated, recreated, desolated
Brave new world

You shouldn't walk that wall, you shouldn't try to call
You shouldn't cry at all, and you shouldn't, you shouldn't fall
You shouldn't walk that way, you shouldn't talk that way
You shouldn't try to say, in a brave new world

ON THE NEWS

On the news last night a catalogue of suffering. But we watch it, night after night, concerned, horrified, indifferent, apathetic, helpless, powerless. Most of us trying to live our lives in peace, a few of us grabbing as much money and power as possible. The psychopaths are not just behind bars, they are in boardrooms too, and on the front benches of parliaments around the world. But we keep breathing and try to pay our bills and watch the world fall apart on TV.

EMPTY OF EXISTENCE

Empty of existence
Still the restless swell
Like an echo of silence
The sea in the shell

THE REAL WORLD *(from the album 'Stranger Place')*

Is it the air defined by a borderline
Is it where they pass real-time
And there's fast food and faster cars
For the cool dudes and the movie stars

An assembly line of future fate
All gift-wrapped in red tape
And inside the pre-paid and packaged lives
All laid out in the nine-to-five
The real world, where is the real world

Is it where daydreams are not allowed
And overhead, a ceiling instead of clouds
And there's income tax and debit loans
For the life inside a credit zone

Is it a place of pride and paedophiles
Where people hide from a stranger's smile
They buy a pager, fax and mobile phone
Don't they ever want to be alone

And they tell me I'm not living in the real world
They don't mean I'm dead
I said if I'm not living in the real world, if I'm not there
Tell me where I am and where is the real world

Is it where truth is scorned as a cliché
And the facts distorted like a fat cat's pay
For all the bad schemes and mad machines
Life as seen on a TV screen

Is it the slick-dick designer lives
And if you don't fit you won't survive
All the sitcoms and atom bombs
Well I think I know where you're coming from

Don't tell me I'm not living in the real world
Cos you don't mean I'm dead but off my head
If I'm not living in the real world, if I'm not there
Tell me where I am and where is the real world

WATCH AND WAIT

We imagine a desert, an endless sea of sand, we imagine heat, a pitiless sun, we imagine wind, gusts of sand in our faces, we imagine oases, palm trees and water, we imagine day and night, birth and death, and it is as real as the ring on my finger, the shoes on my feet, we walk and talk and eat and drink and sleep and dream and die, and all the time we imagine this world and our place in it as something real, something tangible, something true. But it is a fantasy. There is no desert, no sand, no sun, no oasis - not as we see them. They are a reflection of the moon in water, appearing but empty of intrinsic nature. And our nature is likewise appearing but empty, Buddha nature, real, unchanging, pure, ever-present. So in my heart is a great river fed by the rain, drawn to the ocean, always there, always moving, always the same. If I see an ocean not a desert everything changes and yet everything is the same. Watch and wait.

MY MIND IS A MANSION

My mind is a mansion
A million miles wide
And I'm living in the
Front room
Most of the time
But occasionally I get lost
Down dark corridors
Hearing the sound of
Ghostly feet above me
Hurriedly retracing my steps
Until I find myself back
In my comfort zone, that
One room where I have
All my things
All my joy and pain
Safely locked up

WHAT IS REAL?

Writing prose or poems does it really matter what is in my mind is thoughts and feelings and hopes and fears like autumn leaves on or off the trees, trodden underfoot, glorious for a moment before they hit the ground. I am inanimate animation, a car revving with the handbrake on, I am what I am and yet I have songs inside somewhere like eggs waiting to hatch and a dam in my mouth like before. Listen, learn, listen, learn, let the tides turn, they need no pushing or pulling from me, I am not the moon. Thought is mind like a TV, playing pictures, scenes, dramas, images, animate life that is simply a reflection of the moon in water, fundamentally empty, yet appearing. Everything is the TV. Switch it off and the pictures disappear but they still play on other people's TVs in other houses on the street. Is my mind like a TV? This is all an illusion, all mind, but here I am, hiding behind my cushion on the sofa, frightened of the monster in the dark hallway. What is real? Anything?

LUCKY STARS

I don't know her name
Or how near death
She may be
Eyes closed, head laid
Against a hospital pillow
As she's wheeled along
The corridor
A loved one, husband maybe
Walks alongside
And this is the cancer ward
Where so often things
Do not end well
Where so many battles
Are fought, some lost,
Some won
And the lucky ones
Walk away scarred,
Poisoned, cut, radiated
Counting their lucky stars

IN THE GARDEN

Sat in the garden, didn't know why
Gazing at stars with a light in your eyes
You couldn't describe the feeling inside
Couldn't find a reason to try

But outside, life goes on
And outside, there's nothing wrong
Up in the sky and far beyond
In the garden where life, life goes on

Pulled up the weeds, the flowers and all
Went out and bought me some bricks for a wall
And built me a tower to keep it inside
And wait for the thundering storm to subside

Cos outside, life goes on
And outside, there's nothing wrong
Up in the sky and far beyond
In the garden where life, life goes on

His soul is asleep in the seeds that you sow
His essence is there in the flowers you grow
The presence of life in a tree with no name
His absence the arms that are holding your pain

Cos outside, life goes on
And outside, there's nothing wrong
Up in the sky and far beyond
In the garden where life, life goes on

Under the moon, the birds were all sleeping
Softly as you and the willows were weeping
Whispered a prayer seeking hope and a pardon
And listened to silence sing in the garden

START AGAIN

Walking through the autumn leaves, slowly drinking in the sunlight. Time can be as cruel as it is kind. There's no point in writing a book like ' Start Over Again' and then pretending everything is okay. I want to break my heart open, see what's inside. I don't want to be frozen, impale my heart on icicles of fickle feelings that would simply wash away like rain on a river. Yesterday morning felt like the end of the world, but better after a hug and a cup of coffee. If I walk slowly my mind has time to turn and see the sunlight on the grass, to open the door to that secret garden where I used to wander, smelling the flowers, planting seeds, picking fruit. I am the farmer with his empty field spreading manure. But it's not empty, it is full of life underneath the clods of earth and deep, deep down a molten beating heart, the stuff of volcanoes, ready to burst the seeds into next year's harvest, to start again, again.

OVER THE FIELDS

Over the fields where the white gulls wheel
And the brown deer run from you
To the silver sea and the rocky beach
Oh I will walk with you

Over the hills, past the towns and the mills
And the people passing through
Over mountains and streams, through forests of dreams
Oh I will walk with you

Go where the north wind blows
Where the trees grow tall and true
Over the years and the rivers of tears
Oh I will walk with you

Under the stars, under Venus and Mars
In the light of a watchful moon
Near or far you may go down the long winding road
Oh I will walk with you

Go where the north wind blows
Where the trees grow tall and true
Follow the winding road
And I will walk with you

Over the fields where the white gulls wheel
And the brown deer run from you
And then down to the bend to the journey's end
Oh I will walk with you

THE GARDENER

His hands in the earth
The soft thud of the spade
Turning the soil over
New life in the garden
His private domain
Where plants can be cajoled
Trained, nipped, tucked,
Unlike people so uncontrolled
Uncontrollable, in the end

RAINDROPS ON A RIVER

These tears are like raindrops on a river, but there's a wide ocean out there of other people's tears - why are mine special? No reason except here I am, stuck in my skin, hallucinating the days into a dream of what's gone, already gone, and what's to be, that I can't see, waiting for time to tell its story, once upon a time, far, far away. And in my skin, in this fragile jar the cracks start to appear, traces, lines in the glass, this hourglass of sand turned over once more, trickling my life away second by second, the accumulation of my deeds and misdeeds, my futile thoughts and fickle feelings. Read, read, write, write, give me a poem that sucks the blood and tears from my eyes and breaks my heart into a thousand pieces. My heart is small but heavy. I could put my hand down my throat and pull it out, the blood trickling down my chin, and I would hold it in my fists and I would pull, stretch it open wider and wider until it didn't just care for me, for mine, but had enough space inside for everyone whose feet touch the ground, whose heads are full of stars and timebombs, whose hearts are small and heavy but eminently breakable if you dropped them on the cold stone flags. My heart has no name other than mine, my arms bear no weight other than mine. I am the writer, the director, the star and the audience, I am even the stage and the props and the script and the curtains. My life, so easy, so hard to bear. Glue your heart back together, put on a smile, what happened to being light? Always be cheerful. I am a melodramatic, self-absorbed, ignorant fool sleepwalking through my precious human life. Wake up! But I have seen a Buddha, and a rainbow. I know the path is there and I have started walking. It's a long and treacherous route but at least I think I know where I am going. In my darkest moments there has always been light, a glimmer of hope. My breath goes in, and comes out again. And so things change, as they always do, and I start to rise, recover, see a reason for being once more.

THE ROOM

The room has three windows
On two sides
Overlooking fields with horses
She wanted to paint a horse once
Collected photographs
Scraps from magazines
Newspaper cuttings
But somehow became too daunted
Or perhaps just uninspired
Now she can't even make it
To the window
To see the real thing
She sits in her chair
In the corner
Reading books
Dreading the next meal
She's shrinking already
Getting ready for the moment
When death does its
Disappearing trick

IN MY EYES

There's something deep inside of me
That's been there for as long as my memory
But I won't try to express what I could never describe
But in my eyes you'll see the signs to tell you what and why

A restless heart in a rooted breast
Happiness that rests on such a sadness
That I can't cry, I couldn't ever begin to try
Cos in my eyes a wall of tears and not one drop to dry
It would all fall down, melt me down until I'm drowning in my eyes

An unbearable lightness in bearing weight
In an empty vacuum under pressure so great
I've seen the light and I've seen the dark side
I've found the grail and met the devil in disguise
In my eyes

Distilled memories of a fragile past
Fossil senses in a molten cast
Defy my sight, I can't remember what I did last night
But in my eyes it's all true, I've seen through all your lies
But at last I'm a wise fool and the past is paralysed

As unbearable lightness in bearing weight
In an empty vacuum under pressure so great
I've seen the light and I've seen the dark side
I've found the grail and met the devil in disguise
In my eyes

So I'll take an x-ray of my soul's insides
Expose all the things I'd thought it best to hide
In my smile, my mind's a prison with no fair trial
But in my eyes there's a whole horizon open wide
To my blinking, drinking, thinking eyes

WORDS FROM THE ETHER

Drop the storyline. Does it matter to forget? Just put down thoughts, feelings, words from the ether. Exist on the plane detached from the everyday. Dive deeper into the ocean. Don't be afraid to breathe. Do I feel I'll lose the future if I forget the past? Read a book instead of writing this? What am I writing for? To remember, to record, to pin down the past, to sew a tapestry of threads into a picture as the present moment passes, unravelling, always.

STRANGER PLACE *(from the album 'Stranger Place')*

Writing down my changing dreams
They're like waves swelling in a restless sea
The words are cast adrift on scattered reams
They're like debris washed up on a windswept beach
Or so it seems, writing down my changing dreams

Like the tide, my mind changes
And I find my plans in disarray
They're like shattered sandcastles in my brain
And so I build them all again another day and in another way
Cos where there's will there'll always be a way, or so they say

But I can't find the current of my life
I feel I'm constantly swimming against the tide
I'm tossed and turned by each new wave in my face
And each time I find I'm washed up in a stranger place

And I watch the pavement flow beneath my rhythmic feet
I row that river of people passing on the street
The faces floating past belong to worlds not mine
But the bubble lives they don't last for long
And they'll all burst sometime
You know that they must burst sometime, but one time

I must find the current of my life
And not be constantly swimming against the tide
I'm tossed and turned by each new wave in my face
And each time I find I'm washed up in a stranger place

THE LAST TWILIGHT

In the last twilight
We lit a candle to the stars
Left a sign for all our history
A sign for who we are
Then the last bomb dropped
And the silence stopped
Every sound we'd ever heard
Every note and every word
No more hopes, no more dreams
No more money and machines
Just a big black hole
And the chance to begin
At the beginning again

BLACK HOLE

The bright city lights, the faces of the people passing by, a million different stories playing out around me as I walk down the neon-lit street. I could be any one of these people with their preoccupations and their dreams. Are we all sailing on the same sea, or are some of us on rivers, some by waterfalls, some on rapids as we try to steer our lives away from the rocks, into calmer waters, where we can lie back for a while and watch the stars burn in the blackened sky. And know that space is always there, space has no sides, no bottom, no top, no centre, no outside. Like mind. And that gives us hope that we will find our way back home someday. Why hope? Because in a black hole nothing matters, in a black hole is the beginning, in a black hole is life. And where there is life there is possibility and where there is possibility there is hope.

THE POT

I wish I could record
Or at least remember
Half of what you said
As you regarded me
With a smile
Saying "Look, learn, love"
But I am the pot
With a hole at the bottom
You pour in your nectar
And only a drop remains
But in that drop
Lies an ocean
An ocean as blue and
As deep and wide
As your heart
And I can only think
How precious, how privileged
I am to know you
To be the listener
To watch your face
To have your eyes
Shining on me

NOT THE ONLY ONE

I always start the day with good intentions
I'm determined I can find which way to go
But by the afternoon I'm feeling blue
And wondering why the hell I thought I'd ever know
It would be nice, so nice
To be wise, oh wise

If only I could stay a little longer, I think I could change
If I could make my heart a little stronger and rewire my brain
But I'm not the only one trying to find my way

So now I'm standing at this crossroads
My umbrella up and wondering which way to go
I think a signpost could be useful
Or a handle on my suitcase, it's a heavy load
It would be nice, so nice
To travel light, oh light

If only I could stay a little longer, I think I could change
If I could make my heart a little stronger and rewire my brain
But I'm not the only one trying to find my way

Hope fills my eyes in the morning light
Before I am wide awake
And I see my life in black and white
Before it all goes grey
But I don't know why it's been so long
That I've been going wrong

If only I could stay a little longer, I think I could change
If I could make my heart a little stronger and rewire my brain
But I'm not the only one to feel confused
Not the only one feeling blue
Not the only one trying to find my way

SCHOOL

I thought I hated being at school
Teachers telling me what to do
But now I wish I could be told
What I should do as I grow old

GOLDFISH

Turning the tap on is an effort but while the seasons turn and the days spin by what am I really thinking of, beneath the surface? Like the goldfish in a pond, still but vibrant, cocooned in a membrane of water, protected from the deadly air. So what thought or rather what feeling is lying there, in its transient state, a moment before it disappears like a mirage in a desert, just before the real oasis appears over the dunes? Everything has meaning if you let it, but then everything is also empty, empty of what 'it' is. My senses try to make sense of this emptiness, to give it its shape, size, location, colour, smell, taste, touch. To give it meaning - attractive or unattractive - to me. But who am I anyway? A receptor, an automaton, a goldfish in a pond waiting just under the surface for lightning to strike, for the day to begin.

I'D RATHER BE *(from the album 'Believer')*

I would rather be a rolling stone
Than a diamond in a crown
I would rather keep my head in clouds
Than to tie my feet to the ground
And I would rather risk going way too high
Than to never fly at all
I would rather take a running dive
Than be waiting for the fall

I would rather be a restless sea
Than a safely rooted tree
I would rather make it short and sweet
Than to waste a century
And I would rather be a loose cannonball
Than a concrete paradise
I would rather be a waterfall
Than a solid sheet of ice

Cos I would rather be a shooting star
Than the empty space between
I would rather see your face in darkness
Than an ordinary dream
And I would rather take it sweet and slow
Than never bide my borrowed time
I would rather take the highs and lows
Than to hide in a narrow mind

Cos I would rather keep the passion and the pain
Than be chained in sanity
I would rather stand in the pouring rain
To feel the sun shine down on me
Cos I'd rather be free, I'd rather be me

I would rather stare through the blackest night
Than never see the breaking dawn

I would rather bear this rack of life
Than to never have been born
And I would rather be a feeling flying high
Than a reason running down
I would rather be a field of silence
Than a universe of sound

Cos I would rather keep the passion and the pain
Than be chained in sanity
I would rather stand in the pouring rain
To feel the sun shine down on me
Cos I'd rather be free, I'd rather be me

THE VIEW

Every time
I think I want to stop
Something tells me
To keep going
And it's not
That I'm trying
To get somewhere
It's just walking
Is what I do
And along the way
I admire the view

WINDOW

Show me a window onto a wider world, a world full of wonder and possibility, where something amazing is indeed around the corner, and I'm coming round the bend right now, waving my white flag in one hand and my dorje in the other. And of all the questions I could have asked, the answer would always be yes, yes, and I would know all I needed to know to keep breathing, keep smiling, keep walking. Nothing else would matter, moods come and go. I will remember the rainbow, I will remember the moment before the rainbow - the despair, the prayer, the answer. That hope is the seed of confidence. That hope can be strong, not weak, good not bad. Hope says persevere, don't give up, hope says smile, hope says appreciate the good things, hope says things can get better, and they will, hope puts the sun in my heart - better a few shadows than utter darkness. So I say come in to hope, I welcome you and your good intentions and your optimism - why is optimism so much more confident than hope? Because it is hope and confidence combined. Hope plus anxiety equals doubt. Being optimistic means, to me anyway, being cheerfully determined to get your way, to follow your chosen path through the sand, to know that the oasis is real, and you will arrive sometime soon.

RAIN

I'm standing at the railway station
Waiting for the train
And I don't know my destination
Or where I'm gonna stay
Like everyone I'm on the run
I'm just seeking sun and running from
Feeling rain, feeling rain

Cos yesterday the sun was shining
I said I'm gonna stay
But then the storm clouds closed the sky
And I'm on the road again
And every road I've ever run
No I've never caught the sinking sun
And I can't escape from the pouring rain
And I'm here again

And I've got a long way home
And oh the road is lonely
I've been walking alone
The sun will rise and fall again
And I must go, the sun is gone
But the road is long, I can't go on
I'm feeling, feeling rain

Last night I dreamt I was
Standing on the train
Looking out at the city lights
And calling out your name.
Like everyone I'm on the run
I'm just seeking sun, I need someone
To be my refuge from the rain
To make the sun rise again

Cos I've got a long way home
But though the road is lonely
I'm not walking alone
The sun will rise
And I know it must fall again
But I'm not alone, I'm not alone
In feeling, feeling, in feeling rain

HOPE AND HAPPINESS

Wispy white on blue
Above the sound of traffic
A seagull cries
Down by the sea
Waves still come and go
Here in my attic
My moods still come and go
One more pill to pin
My feet to the ground
As you can tell
I've not much in the way of words
But I'm writing anyway
I guess it's the habit
That breeds its own progeny
And I'm rusty
But starting always means
A moment after the moment
Before when you were still
Thinking about what to do
What to say
A cavern in your mind
Where once there was treasure
But now seems black and empty
So I start again
Think of how to enjoy this day
With its blue sky and its
Humming traffic and all its potential for
Hope and happiness
Even for me

TIME TO GO

I've always wanted to know the right answer, to see the world in black and white. But life is not monochrome, there's a million shades of grey, and such mystery is all we need to feel there is something more - that I could climb this hill and on the other side would be another world, that I could reach the horizon, that there are more questions than answers, and all we need to do is ask. And all I need to do is start walking. I don't know the destination, I only know it's time to go.

www.emilymaguire.com

INDEX